RUNNING PRESS

GEM

GREAT GAMES

*More Than 200 Games
for All Ages*

The Diagram Group

S0-AFN-842

Running Press
Philadelphia, Pennsylvania

First published in the United States of America in 1994 by
Running Press Book Publishers.

Copyright © 1990, 1994 by Diagram Visual Information Ltd

Originally published by HarperCollins Publishers Limited under the
title *Collins Gem Family and Party Games*

9 8 7 6 5 4 3 2 1
Digit on the right indicates the number of this printing.

ISBN: 1-56138-383-X

Library of Congress Cataloging-in-Publication Number: 93-085522

Cover design by Toby Schmidt

Printed in Italy by Amadeus S.p.A.

This book may be ordered by mail from your publisher. Please
include $2.50 for postage and handling. *But try your bookstore first!*

Running Press Book Publishers
125 South Twenty-second Street
Philadelphia, Pennsylvania 19103-4399

Introduction

Games for the car? A children's party? A family
celebration? What shall we do at Christmas? How
do you play chess? What height should a darts
board be? A new variation on solitaire? How can I
make the family laugh? What is Plakato? What
country did Backgammon come from?

You will find the answers to these questions about
games for family occasions – and many, many more
– inside. Over 260 games are clearly described and
often illustrated with diagrams, drawings and
situations. All the old favorites from your own
childhood are here, brought up to date. This book
dispels boredom.

Contents

How many players?

These lists show at a glance which games are
suitable for one, two, three or four players, for
groups of varying size.

GAMES FOR THREE PLAYERS

Board games (race)
Ludo 237
Tiddlywinks 146–151
Dice games
Round the clock

Tile games
Dominoes:
  All fives 164
  All threes 166
  Bergen 168
  Fives and threes 166

GAMES FOR FOUR PLAYERS

Board games (race)
Ludo 237
Dice games
Round the clock 128
Tile games
Dominoes:
  All fives 164

Bergen 168
Block (partnership) 159
Fortress/Sebastopol,
Cyprus 163
Forty-two 169
Latin American
match 160

GAMES FOR TWO OR MORE PLAYERS

Note that many of these games become impracticable
for groups of more than seven or eight players
Board games (race)
Snakes and ladders 240
Dice games
Basketball 193
Beetle 131
Centennial 133
Cheerio 139
Chicago 128
Double Cameroon 144
Drop dead 128
Fifty 126
General 142

Hearts 133
Pig 129
Shut the box 126
Target games
Darts: 180
  Around the clock 184
  Cricket 189
  Halve it 188
  Killer 185
  Shanghai 184
Pick-up-sticks 153
Spellicans 152

OTHER GAMES FOR GROUPS

All these games can be played by quite large groups.

Alphabetical list of games

Blindfold

In these games, the blindfolded player's movements are a source of much amusement. It is a good idea if an adult ties on the blindfold and checks that it is tied neither so tightly as to be painful nor so loosely that the "blind man" can peep out.

BLIND MAN'S BLUFF

Objective A blindfolded player tries to catch and identify another player.

Play A blind man is chosen and blindfolded. He is turned around three times in the center of the room and then left on his own.

The other players dance around, taunting him and dodging out of his way to avoid capture.

When the blind man catches someone, he has two or three guesses at the name of his prisoner. If he guesses correctly, the prisoner becomes the new blind man. If wrong, he continues to be the blind man and tries to catch another player.

TEN STEP BLUFF

Objective As in Blind man's bluff, a blindfolded player tries to catch and identify another player.

Play The blind man stands in the center of the room. The other players scatter around him and stand still.

The blind man takes ten steps and stretches out his hands. If he touches a player, that player becomes the blind man. If not, he takes another ten steps and tries again.

SQUEAK-PIGGY-SQUEAK

Objective A blindfolded player attempts to identify another player by getting him to squeak.

Play One player is blindfolded, given a cushion, and turned around three times in the center of the room. The others sit down around the room. The blind man must then place his cushion on another player's lap and sit on it. He then calls "squeak-piggy-squeak" and the person he is sitting on squeaks like a pig. If the blind man recognizes the person, he changes places with him. Once the new person is blindfolded, the players all change seats before he tries to sit on a player's lap.

BLIND MAN'S STICK

Objective A blind man tries to identify a player from the noises he makes.

Play One player is blindfolded and given a stick. The others from a circle and slowly move around him.

If the blind man touches a player with his stick, the player must grasp the stick. The blind man then asks the player to imitate a noise – for example a creaking door.

If the blind man guesses the player's name, that player becomes the new blind man. If he guesses incorrectly, the blind man must touch another player.

BLIND JUDGEMENT

Play One player is blindfolded and placed on a "seat of judgment."

Another player then stands quietly in front of him, and the player in the judgment seat gives a brief description of whoever he thinks might be standing in front of him.

If the other players think that the "blind judgment" was reasonably accurate, the player in front of the blindfolded player becomes the new blind man.

If his judgment was inaccurate, the original blind man must pass judgment on another player.

BLIND MAN'S TREASURE HUNT

This game is an excellent way of giving out small presents at a party.

Objective Each player chooses a parcel by touch and tries to identify the contents before opening it.

Preparation Objects of different shape and feel are wrapped up – one parcel per player. The parcels are piled on a table.

Play Each player in turn is blindfolded and led to the table to choose a parcel. He then takes off his blindfold and waits until all the players have chosen a parcel. Each player then guesses what is in his parcel before opening it.

BLIND POSTMAN

Objective A blindfolded player tries to sit in a vacant seat while two players are changing places.

Preparation One person is chosen to be postmaster. All the others choose a town, and the postmaster makes a list of their choices.

Play One player is blindfolded and becomes the first postman. All the other players sit in a circle. The postman stands in the center of the circle, and is turned around several times by the postmaster.

The postmaster then announces that a letter has been sent between two of the towns on his list, for example from New York to Chicago. The two players whose towns are called then try to change places before the postman sits in one of their empty seats.

If the postman gets a seat, the player without a seat becomes the new postman. More than one letter may be sent at a time.

Mode of travel The postmaster can also say how the letter traveled – and so indicate how the players should move. For example, if the letter went:

(a) by air, they hop;

(b) by sea, they walk backwards;

(c) by train, they crawl; and

(d) by Pony Express, they bunny hop.

THIEVES

Objective A blindfolded player tries to catch players stealing from him.

Play One player is blindfolded and given a rolled newspaper to hold in his hand.

The blindfolded player sits in the middle of a circle made by the other players, and a pile of treasure – necklaces, brooches, bracelets, etc. – is placed in front of him.

Players in the circle quietly take it in turns to steal a piece of treasure. If the blind man hears a thief, he strikes at him with the newspaper and calls "thief, thief."

If he touches a thief, the thief must return empty-handed to his place to await the next turn. The thief who collects most treasure wins the game.

JAILER

This is similar to Thieves except that the
blindfolded man is guarding a bunch of keys.
The organizer names a player, who then has to take
the keys from the jailer and carry them around the
outside of the circle and back to his place.
The jailer listens for the thief and if he hears him
points at him. If the jailer locates the thief, the thief
takes over as jailer.

PIN THE TAIL ON THE DONKEY

Objective Blindfolded players try to pin a tail in the
correct position on a drawing of a tail-less donkey.

Preparation The organizer draws a large picture of
a donkey without a tail and fastens it onto a
pinboard propped upright. He also makes a
donkey's tail out of cardboard or wool and sticks a
large pin through the body end.

Play Each player in turn is blindfolded and turned
around so that he is in front of and facing the
donkey. He is then given the tail and attempts to pin
it on the correct part of the donkey.
The organizer marks the position of each player's
attempt. The player who pins nearest the correct
place is the winner.

ELEPHANT'S TAIL

This is similar to Pin the Tail on the Donkey but
instead of pinning on a tail, players draw one. Each
blindfolded player is given a crayon and draws a tail
on a picture of an elephant (or any other animal).

MURALS

Preparation The organizer cuts out large pieces of
paper for drawing on.

Play Each player in turn is blindfolded, given a crayon, and asked to draw a picture on a piece of paper pinned to the wall. The subject of the picture is chosen by the other players – good examples are a house, a person or some kind of animal.

The artist feels the edges of the paper and has one minute in which to draw the chosen subject. When everyone has had a turn, the drawings can be judged by an adult or by all the players together.

SWEET TOOTH

Objective Each player tries to identify foods that he has eaten while blindfolded.

Play Each player sits down and is then provided with a plate of food such as chocolate, fudge, nuts, licorice and pieces of orange.

When all the players have eaten or tasted all their foods, any leftovers are taken away and the blindfolds are removed.

The players then write down what they think they have eaten. If the players are too young to write, they can whisper their answers to an adult.

BLIND MAN'S SORT OUT

Objective Blindfolded players race to sort a collection of objects into categories.

Preparation The organizer collects a selection of buttons, screws, nails, beans, beads, etc.

Play The game is usually organized as an elimination contest – with two players competing at a time.

The objects are divided into two similar piles. The first two players are then blindfolded and each is placed in front of a pile of objects.

When the organizer calls "Go!" each of the
blindfolded players start sorting his objects into
groups of buttons, screws, etc. The first player to
finish sorting his objects into categories advances
to the next round of the contest.

All the other players then compete in pairs, and
the winners all go into the next round.

Further rounds are held until only two players
remain for the final. The winner of the final wins
the game.

NELSON'S EYE

This game plays on a blindfolded person's
heightened imagination.

Play Several volunteers who do not already know
the game are asked to leave the room. They are
blindfolded and brought back into the room one at
a time.

One of the other players begins by asking the blind
man to feel "Nelson's good leg" – and the blind
mans hands are guided so that he can feel
someone's leg.

He is then asked to feel Nelson's bad leg – and his
hands are guided to a chair leg.

Next the blind man must feel Nelson's good arm –
and feels someone's arm. Then he must feel
Nelson's bad arm, which can be a stuffed sock. This
is followed by Nelson's good eye, which can be a
marble. Finally, he is asked to feel Nelson's bad eye
– and is presented with a squashy peeled grape or a
soft flour and water mixture. The blind man usually
becomes rather squeamish at this point – much to
the amusement of the other players!

BLINDFOLD OBSTACLE WALK

Preparation Everyone lays out obstacles – a pile of books, a glass of water, cushions, etc. – from one end of the room to the other.

Play Several of the players volunteer to walk the course. They then leave the room to be blindfolded. Meanwhile the others quickly and quietly remove all the obstacles.

Each of the blindfolded volunteers is then brought in one at a time.

The blindfolded player then attempts to walk across the room without hitting the obstacles. To add to the fun, all the onlookers utter appropriate gasps and shudders.

When he has completed the "course" the blindfold is removed.

MURDER IN THE DARK

Although players are not blindfolded for this game, a "detective" attempts to identify an unseen "murderer." The opening stages of play take place in the dark.

Preparation One small piece of paper per player is folded and placed in a hat. One is marked with a cross, another with a D, and all the others are blank.

Play Each player draws a piece of paper from the hat. The player who gets the paper with the cross is the murderer and the one with the D the detective. The detective first leaves the room and the lights are switched off.

The other players then move slowly around the room in the dark. The murderer catches a victim and puts his hands on the victim's shoulders. The victim must scream and fall to the ground. The lights are then switched on and the detective is called in.

The detective tries to identify the murderer by questioning everybody except the victim. All the players except the murderer must answer his questions truthfully.

After the questioning the detective accuses his prime suspect of the murder, saying "I charge you (name of suspect) with the murder of (name of victim)." If the accusation is correct, the murderer must admit his guilt.

Balloon flights

Contests

In these games, players perform various feats of skill. Some of the games are a test of physical strength or ability, others need ingenuity in order to outwit opponents. It is a good idea in case of dispute for someone to act as a referee.

BALLOON FLIGHTS

Objective Each player tries to flick a balloon the farthest distance.

Play Players form a straight line. Each person balances a balloon on the palm of one hand. Balloons should all be a different color, or marked with the players' initials.

The referee counts "One, two, three, go," and each player then flicks his balloon with the first finger and thumb of his other hand. The player whose balloon makes the longest flight is the winner.

STATIC ELECTRICITY

Objective Each player tries to have the most balloons sticking to a wall at the end of a time limit.

Preparation Plenty of balloons are inflated and their necks tied.

Play The balloons are placed in a pile in the center of the room and each player is allocated an area of wall.

On the word "Go," each player takes a balloon, rubs it on his clothing to create static electricity, and then tries to make it stick to the wall.

If he succeeds, he takes another balloon and does

the same, and so on with as many balloons as possible. If the balloon falls off the wall any player may use it again.

End At the end of a time limit, the player with the most balloons still sticking to the wall wins.

HOPPIT

Objective Each player tries to hop the farthest while making progressively larger hops.

Play Using strands of wool, two straight lines are marked on the floor. The lines are about 1ft. (30cm.) apart at one end of the room and fan out to about 5ft. (1.5m.) apart at the other.

Players take turns at hopping back and forth across the two lines. They start at the narrow end and move down the room. The player who gets the farthest down the line before failing to hop right across the two lines, is the winner.

SINGING HIGH JUMP

This is a test of vocal range – each player aims to sing the most widely spaced low and high notes.

Play The referee stands by a "take-off" line ready to score each players attempt.

In turn, each player runs up to the take-off line, stops, and sings two notes: the first as low as possible, the second as high as possible. The player who makes the highest musical "jump" is the winner.

APPLE ON A STRING

This game is an old favorite for Hallowe'en. Players try, without using their hands, to eat apples suspended from strings.

Play A piece of string is hung across the room,

well above head height. One apple (or doughnut) per person is suspended from it, also on a string. The players try to eat their apples or doughnuts without using their hands. The first player to eat the apple down to its core, or to finish eating the doughnut, is the winner.

APPLE PARING

Objective Each player tries to peel the longest unbroken paring from an apple.

Play Each player is given an apple, a knife, and a plate. All the apples and all the knives should be of similar quality.

The players then peel their apples. The winner is the one to produce the longest and narrowest paring.

SWEET WRAPPER

The game is similar to apple paring, but instead of fruit the players get a sweet to eat.

Objective Each player aims to tear a sweet wrapper into a long, thin, spiral strip.

Play Each player is given a sweet, which he unwraps. While eating the sweet, he tears its wrapping paper, starting at the outer edge and tearing round and round towards the center. The player with the longest unbroken strip of paper wins.

HAPPY TRAVELERS

Each player tries to be the first to sort the pages of a newspaper into the correct order.

Preparation For each player the pages of a newspaper are put together in the wrong order – some pages may be upside down or back to front –

and then folded.

Play Players sit facing each other in two rows.
They should sit very close together like passengers
on a crowded train.

Each player is given one of the newspapers. On the
word "Go!" each player tries to rearrange the
pages of his newspaper into the correct order. The
first player to succeed wins the game.

PRINTERS' ERRORS

In this game, players try to set out jumbled lines of
a printed article into their correct order.

Preparation A jumbled article is needed for each
player. The organizer makes as many copies of the
article as he needs and then jumbles each one by
cutting it into pieces after each line.

Play Each player is given his jumbled article.
When the organizer gives the signal players start to
sort out their article. The winner is the first player
to put his article into the correct order.

CARD AND BUCKET CONTEST

Objective Players try to flick all their cards into a
bucket or other large container.

Play Each player is given ten playing cards –
preferably old ones – and writes down which ones
they are.

The players then form a large circle around a
bucket. On the call of "Go!" each player tries to
flick his cards into the bucket.

When all the players have flicked all their cards,
the cards in the bucket are identified.

The winner is the player who gets most cards into
the bucket. Several rounds may be played.

GRANDMOTHERS FOOTSTEPS

Objective Each player tries to be the first one to creep up behind the "grandmother" without her seeing him move.

Play One person is chosen as the grandmother and stands, with shut eyes, facing a wall.

The other players line up against the opposite wall. When everyone is ready, the players start to creep up behind the grandmother – but whenever she looks round they must "freeze" into statues.

The grandmother may look round as often as she likes. If she sees anyone moving, she points to him and he has to go back to the start. The grandmother turns round to face the wall, and the players move forwards again.

The first player to touch the grandmother's wall wins – and takes the next turn at being grandmother.

LIMBO

Originally a West Indian acrobatic dance, this is a test of suppleness and sustained contortion.

Play Two people gently hold a long stick horizontally and at chest height.

Each player in turn bends backward and edges himself under the stick. He must neither touch the floor with his hands nor touch the stick.

If a player, after two attempts, fails to pass under the stick he is eliminated. After each round, the stick is lowered a little. The last person to stay in the game is the winner.

TWO-MINUTE WALK

Objective Each player tries to walk from one end

of the room to the other in exactly two minutes.

Play Players line up along one wall. On the word "Go!" they set off across the room. Without using a watch or a clock, each player tries to reach the other side of the room in exactly two minutes. The organizer times the players' walks.

When all the players have finished, the player whose time was nearest two minutes wins.

RUMORS

This is a competitive form of the popular old game of Chinese telephone.

Objective Each player tries to pass on a message that has been whispered to him.

Play Players divide into two equal teams and each team sits down in a circle. Players take it in turns to be team leader. The organizer decides on a message and whispers it to the two leaders.

Each leader then whispers the message to the player to his right. This player then whispers the message as he heard it to the player to his right, and so on around the circle. Whisperers are not allowed to give the message more than once.

The last player of each team tells the leader the message as he heard it. The leader then tells the message as it began. The team that relayed the message most accurately wins the game.

STORK-FIGHTING CONTEST

Play Two players tie their left ankles together with a scarf, and hop on their right feet.

Each player then tries to make his opponent's left foot touch the ground – without putting down his own left foot.

If a players left foot touches the ground, his
opponent scores a point.
The winner is the player with the most points at the
end of a time limit.

COCK-FIGHTING CONTEST

Play Two players crouch on the floor facing each
other.
Each brings his knees together under his chin and
clasps his legs with his arms. A stick is then passed
under his knees and over his arms.
The two players then try to tip each other over.
The first player to succeed in making his opponent
fall over is the winner.

ARM WRESTLING

Play Two players sit facing each other at either
side of a table. Resting their right elbows on the
table and with crooked arms, they clasp each
other's right hands. (Both players may use their left
arms if they prefer.)
On the signal to begin, each player tries to force his
opponent's right hand back until it touches the
table. Elbows must be kept firmly on the table. The
winner is the first to succeed.

Arm wrestling

Goal Scoring

Although goal scoring games are often based on
energetic outdoor sports, they can safely be played
in the home if a balloon, soft ball, or large rag is
used. Playing with balloons is particularly enjoyable
as they are difficult to control and unlikely to cause
damage.

AVENUE GOALS

Players try to score goals by patting a ball or
balloon so that it goes beyond their opponents' end
of the avenue.

Players The players form two lines about 5ft.
(1.5m.) apart, and sit or kneel facing each other on
the floor. Counting from one end, the odd-
numbered players in one line belong to the same
team as the even-numbered players in the other
line.

Each team is assigned one end of the avenue as its
goal.

Play The organizer puts the ball into the center of
the avenue. Each team tries to score by patting the
ball by hand down the avenue into his opponent's
goal. Players are not allowed to hold or throw the
ball. The ball is put back into the center of the
avenue after each goal. The winning team is the one
with most goals at the end of a time limit.

OVERHEAD GOALS

Players try to score goals by patting a balloon over
their opponents' heads.

Players The players form two teams in rows about 4ft. (1.2m.) apart, and sit facing each other on the floor.

Play The organizer tosses the balloons into the center.

Each team tries to score goals by knocking the balloon over the heads of the opposing team and onto the ground behind them. The winning team is the one with most goals at the end of a time limit.

BALLOON VOLLEYBALL

In Balloon volleyball, players hit a balloon over a piece of string held taut by two players standing on chairs.

Players The players divide into two teams, one on either side of the string. Players within a team take turns at serving (hitting the balloon into play at the start of play or after a break).

Play Players hit the balloon back and forth over the string and with the aim of making a shot that their opponents will not be able to return.

A team scores a point whenever it hits the balloon over the string and onto the floor on its opponent's side. If the ball goes under the string, the opposing team serves it.

The winning team is the one with most points at the end of a time limit.

BLOW VOLLEYBALL

This is played in exactly the same way as Balloon volleyball except that the balloon is blown rather than hit, and the string is held lower.

ASTRIDE BALL

This is a goal-scoring game without teams.

Players One player stands in the center of a circle formed by the other players standing with their legs apart.

Play The center player has a ball to be rolled along the ground. If he rolls it between the legs of a player in the circle, he "scores a goal" and changes places with that player.

The players in the circle should keep their hands on their knees except when trying to prevent a goal.

HOCKEY RAG TIME

In this game, team members take turns at trying to shoot a goal.

Players The players form two rows about 6ft. (1.8m.) apart and sit facing each other on the floor. Each team member is given a number, starting with one. A rag and two sticks are laid on the floor between the two rows of players. A chair is placed at each end of the avenue as a goal. Each team is allotted one of the goals.

Play The organizer calls out a number. Each player with that number picks up a stick and uses it to maneuvre the rag into his opponent's goal. The successful player scores a point for his side.

The rag and sticks are replaced and the organizer calls another number.

The winning team is the one with the most goals at the end of a time limit.

Musical

These are all active games in which players move around to music. When the music stops, the players must immediately stand still or change what they are doing. All the games require someone to organize the music.

MUSICAL CHAIRS
Preparation Chairs are placed around the room in a large circle. There should be one chair fewer than the number of players.
Play The players stand in the circle and, when the music starts, all dance around.
When the music stops, each player tries to sit on a seat. The player left without a seat is eliminated. One chair is then removed from the circle and the music is restarted. The last person to stay in the game is the winner.

MUSICAL STATUES
This game is an enjoyable "quiet" alternative to Musical chairs.
Play Players dance around the room to music. When the music stops, the players immediately stop dancing and stand as still as statues.
Any player seen moving after the music stops is out.
The music is started again fairly quickly and the game continues.
Eliminated players can help to spot moving statues. The last player to remain as a dancer is the winner.

MUSICAL BUMPS

This is like Musical chairs, except that it is played without the chairs. When the music stops, players sit down on the floor. The last person to sit down is out.

OWNERSHIP MUSICAL CHAIRS

In this version of Musical chairs, there is one chair per person. Before the music starts each player sits on a chair and marks it as his own.

When the music starts, the players dance around the circle in the same direction.

When the music stops, the players continue moving around the circle. As each player comes to his own chair he sits down. The last player to sit on his chair is out and remains seated.

The organizer may vary the game by calling directions to the players as they move around – e.g. walk backwards, or turn to the right.

The last person to stay in the game is the winner.

MUSICAL BLACKOUT

This is played like Musical chairs except that when the music stops, the lights are switched off for five seconds. When the lights are switched on again, any player who has not found a chair is out.

HIGH STEPPERS

Preparation Pairs of chairs with their fronts touching are placed around the room to form a circle of hurdles.

Play The players space themselves around the room in pairs. When the music starts, they march around the room and must climb over the hurdles as they come to them. When the music stops, any

pair touching a hurdle is out. The music starts
again and the game continues. The winning pair is
the last one left in the game.

MUSICAL HOTCHPOTCH

In this game, players race for objects instead of
chairs.

Preparation A pile of objects, numbering one
fewer than the number of players, is placed in the
center of the room.

Play When the music starts, players hop or dance
around the pile.

When the music stops, each player dives for an
article from the pile. The larger the objects, the less
likely are the players to bump their heads!

The player left without an object is out. One object
is removed from the pile and the game continues.

MUSICAL ISLANDS

Preparation Small mats, newspapers, pieces of
cardboard, etc., are scattered over the floor to form
"islands."

Play When the music starts, players walk around
in a circle. When the music stops, players must
stand on an island. More than one player may
stand on one island.

Anyone unable to get onto an island or falling off
into the "water" is eliminated. The music starts
again and the game continues.

Islands are gradually removed during the game.
The last player left in the game is the winner.

Observation

In addition to games of pure observation, such as Memory game, this group also includes a wide variety of hunting games. Many hunting games involve searching for hidden objects, whereas in Hide and seek and its entertaining alternative Sardines it is other players who must be hunted.

MEMORY GAME
Sometimes called Memory test or Kim's game, this is an excellent test of the players' powers of observation.

Preparation The organizer puts about 20 small objects on a tray. He then covers them with a cloth until play begins.

Kim's game

Play The organizer uncovers the object and allows the players about 3 minutes in which to memorize them. The players are not allowed to make any notes.

At the end of the time limit, the organizer removes the tray and gives each player a pencil and paper. The players are then asked to write down as many of the objects as they can. The winner is the player who remembers the most objects.

MISMATCHES

This is a team observation game, in which the team tries to spot all the "mismatches" made by the other.

Play Players divide into two teams. One team leaves the room while the other makes its mismatches by altering things in the room.

For example, the team making the mismatches might change the position of objects – such as turning a vase upside down – or might change something about a person – such as putting a cardigan on inside out.

At the end of a time limit, the other team returns and tries to spot the mismatches. At the end of another time limit, any mismatches that have not been noticed score one point to the team that made them.

The team then change roles, and the winning team is the team that scores most points.

WRONG!

In this game players try to spot deliberate errors in a story that is read to them.

Preparation The organizer writes a short story in which there are numerous errors of fact – for example, he might say that he went to the antique shop and bought a new clock.

Play The organizer reads out the story. If a player spots a mistake he shouts "Wrong!" The first player to call out a mistake scores one point. A player who shouts when there has been no mistake loses one point. The player with most points at the end of the story wins the game.

CUT-OUT PAIRS

This is a good game for introducing players to each other at the start of a party.

Preparation All sorts of pictures are cut out of magazines, comics, etc. Each picture is pasted onto cardboard and cut into two oddly shaped pieces. (Postcards may be used to save time.) There should be one picture for each pair of players.

Play Each player is given one piece of a picture. He then tries to find the player with the other half of the same picture.

When two players have a complete picture they write a suitable caption for it. Pictures and captions are displayed and the writers of the funniest caption may win a prize.

MOTHERS AND BABIES

This is another pairing game along the lines of Cut-out pairs. For this game, players are given a card showing a mother or a baby animal – for example, a cow or a calf, a frog or a tadpole. Players then have to find the player with the card showing the other member of their family.

HUNT THE SLIPPER

In this game one player tries to find which of the others is holding the slipper. A little acting greatly adds to the fun.

Play All the players but one sit with their feet touching in a circle on the floor. These players are the cobblers.

The other player has a small slipper (or shoe) which he says is in need of repair. He then gives the slipper to the cobblers and asks them to mend it. He walks away and returns several times to see if it is ready. Each time the cobblers pretend that it is not quite finished. Finally, however, they admit that they have lost it.

The hunt The cobblers now pass the slipper from one to another under their knees. The customer tries to touch a cobbler while he is holding the slipper. When he succeeds, the slipper is "found" and the customer and the cobbler holding the slipper change places.

HUNT THE RING

This is another game in which one player tries to find which of the others is holding an object.

Preparation A curtain ring is threaded onto a long piece of string. The two ends of the string are then tied together with a knot that is small enough to allow the ring to pass easily over it.

Play One player stands in the middle of the room and the others form a circle around him. The players in the circle each hold the string with both hands – and one of them also holds the ring so that the player in the middle cannot see it. When the player in the middle says "Go!" the others pass the string through their hands – passing the ring from hand to hand at the same time.

The player in the center tries to locate the ring by touching any hand he thinks conceals it. A player must open his hand if it is touched. If it concealed the ring, he must change places with the player in the center. If his hand is empty, the original player stays in the middle.

UP JENKINS!

This game is similar to Hunt the ring but is played with any small object instead of a ring on a string.

Play On player sits on the floor in the middle of a circle formed by the other players sitting around him. The players in the circle sit with their hands behind their backs and one of them holds the small object.

When the player in the middle says "Go!" the players in the circle all pass, or pretend to pass, the object around the circle behind their backs.

When the player in the middle says "Up Jenkins!" the players in the circle, including the one with the object, must all raise their clenched fists.

When the player in the middle says "Down Jenkins!" the players in the circle must put their hands palms down on the ground – and the player with the object must, of course, do his best to keep the object concealed at this stage of the game. The player in the middle then tries to identify which of the players is hiding the object.

HUNT THE THIMBLE

This very popular game is usually played with a

thimble, but any other small object will do just as well.

Play All the players but one leave the room while this player hides the thimble somewhere in the room or on his person. He then calls the other players back into the room to look for it.

The game is won by the first player to find the thimble and take it to the player who hid it. The finder then has a turn at hiding the thimble.

SIT DOWN HUNT THE THIMBLE

This is played in the same way as the last game except that when a player sees where the thimble is hidden he sits down on the floor.

The last person to see the thimble and sit down must pay a forfeit. The player who sat down first has the next turn at hiding the thimble.

SINGING HUNT THE THIMBLE

This is played like Hunt the thimble except that only one player leaves the room while one of the others hides it.

On his return, the players who stayed in the room try to guide him to the thimble by singing. They sing more loudly as he moves closer to the thimble and more quietly as he moves away.

HOT AND COLD THIMBLE

As in Singing hunt the thimble, only one player leaves the room while the thimble is hidden.

The other players help him find the thimble by telling him how "hot" he is in different parts of the room. If he is in the wrong part of the room he is "very cold" or "cold." As he approaches the thimble he is "getting warmer" – until he becomes "warm," "hot," and finally "very hot" just before he touches the thimble.

BEAN HUNT

Preparation The organizer hides a large quantity of beans around the room. A small container such as a paper cup is needed for each player.

Play Each player collects as many beans as he can within a given time limit. The player who finds most beans is the winner.

BUTTERFLY HUNT

This game is played in the same way as Bean hunt except that players look for paper butterflies hidden by the organizer. The winner is the player who finds most butterflies after an agreed time limit.

JIGSAW HUNT

Preparation One "jigsaw" is needed for each player. The organizer makes the jigsaws by cutting postcards into four irregular pieces. Three pieces from each jigsaw are hidden in the room.

Play Each player is given one of the jigsaw pieces that was not hidden. The first player to find the three pieces missing from his jigsaw wins the game.

PRESENT HUNT

Each player is given a piece of paper with a written clue to guide him to his present.

COLOR HUNT

This game is played in the same way as Present hunt except that each player is given a small piece of wrapping paper and then hunts for and keeps the present wrapped in the same sort of paper.

EASTER EGG HUNT

Each player hunts for a chocolate Easter egg wrapped in a particular color of paper.

Alternatively, a tag with the name of one of the players may be attached to each hidden egg.

CARD HUNT

In this game, players form two teams and look for playing cards hidden around the room.

Preparation Two decks of playing cards are needed. The cards from one deck are hidden around the room within reach of the players. The other deck is divided into two piles – one of red cards and one of black cards.

Play Each member of one team is given a black card and each member of the other team is given a red one.

Each player searches for the hidden card that matches the card he has been given. When a player finds the card he is looking for he takes it to the organizer who gives him another card of the same color.

Play continues in this way until one of the teams has found all its cards.

HIDDEN OBJECTS

In this game players look for objects hidden all around the house.

Preparation The organizer hides about 20 objects in different rooms. It should be possible to see the objects without moving anything. A list of the objects is prepared for each of the players.

Play Each player is given a list and tries to locate the objects, noting down wherever he finds one. The game is won by the first player to locate all the objects and take his list to the organizer.

SCAVENGER HUNT

This game requires more preparation and ingenuity than most hunting games.

Preparation The organizer draws up a series of clues in such a way that the solution of each clue will lead players to the hiding place of the next one. The solution of the last clue may lead to:

(a) a prize for the first player or pair to find it;

(b) a pile of presents, one for each player; or

(c) the table set with the party food.

Play Sometimes players take part on their own. Alternatively, they may play in pairs.

The organizer gives each player or pair the first clue. As the other clues are discovered, they should be left in their places for the other players to find.

STOREKEEPERS

This is an enjoyable team hunting game. It is best if there are about four teams each with three or four members. Each team represents a different store.

Preparation The organizer takes a number of plain cards and writes the name of a commodity on each one. These commodities should be items sold in the stores that will be represented. There should be an equal number of cards for each store. These cards are hidden around the room.

Play The players form teams and each team is given the name of a store – for example, the bakery

or the grocery store. The players are told how
many commodities are missing from the store.
Each team chooses a "storekeeper," who stands in
the middle of the room. The other players then
look for the cards and when they find a card for
their own store take it to their storekeeper.
The game is won by the team that first finds all its
hidden commodities.

SARDINES

This is a type of Hide and seek (see below) usually
played in the dark. The more rooms that can be
played in the more exciting the game becomes.

Play One player is chosen as the first sardine. He
then leaves the room and finds a place to hide –
preferably somewhere big enough for most of the
others to squeeze in, too.
When the first sardine has had time to hide, the
other players split up and look for him. When a
player finds the hiding place he creeps in and hides
with the first sardine.
The last sardine to find the others usually becomes
the first sardine for the next game.

HIDE AND SEEK

Children enjoy organizing this game themselves.

Play Players choose somewhere to be "home" –
for example a chair or a door. They also choose
someone to be the first "seeker." The seeker then
shuts his eyes and counts to 40 while all the other
players hide.
When he reaches 40, he shouts "Ready or not here
I come!" and goes and looks for the other players.
When he finds a player, that player must try to

reach home before the seeker can touch him. The first player to be touched on the way home becomes the next seeker.

Hide and seek

Parcel

Everyone loves to unwrap a parcel to find a present
inside. Pass the parcel is an old favorite and is
enjoyed by children of all ages. There are also a
number of entertaining variations on the parcel-
opening theme.

PASS THE PARCEL

Preparation A small present is wrapped in layer
after layer of paper. Each layer should be secured
with thread, glue, or a rubber band. Music – to be
started and stopped by someone not taking part in
the game – is also needed.

Play Players sit in a circle and one of them holds
the parcel. When the music starts, players pass the
parcel around the circle to the right.

When the music stops whoever is holding the parcel
unwraps one layer of wrapping. The music is then
restarted and the parcel passed on again.

The game continues in this way until someone takes
off the final wrapping and so wins the present.

FORFEITS PARCEL

This game is the same as Pass the parcel except that
a forfeit is written on each layer of wrapping. A
player who is holding the parcel when the music
stops must carry out the next forfeit before taking
off the next layer of wrapping.

MYSTERY PARCEL

Preparation A parcel is prepared as for Pass the
parcel but with a message written on each layer of

wrapping. Typical messages are "Give to the player with the whitest teeth!" and "Pass to the person to your left!" Music is needed.

Play The parcel is passed around to the music as in Pass the parcel. When the music stops, the player holding the parcel reads out the message and hands the parcel to the player who fits the description in the message. This player then unwraps the next layer of paper before the music is restarted.

HOT POTATO

Preparation A present is given a single strong wrapper. Music is needed.

Play is as for Pass the parcel except that when the music stops the person holding the parcel drops out of the game. The last player left in the game unwraps the parcel and wins the present.

LUCKY CHOCOLATE GAME

Preparation A chocolate bar is wrapped in several layers of paper. Each layer should be secured with thread.

The parcel and a knife and fork are then put on a breadboard on a table. A chair with a hat, scarf and gloves on it is then placed at the table. One die is also needed.

Play The players sit in a circle on the floor and take it in turns to throw the die.

If a player throws a 6, he puts on the hat, scarf and gloves, sits on the chair and uses the knife and fork to remove the wrappings.

If another player throws a 6, he changes places with the player at the table.

When the chocolate is unwrapped, players at the table use the knife and fork to eat one piece of the chocolate. The game continues until all the chocolate has been eaten.

Lucky chocolate game

Trickery

In these games, players try to trick others into carrying out some action for which they will be penalized. The usual penalty in most of these games is for a player to drop out if he makes a mistake. Alternatively, players may be allowed to stay in the game if they carry out a forfeit.

MY LITTLE BIRD

This game is played in countries all over the world. Other names for it include Flying high and Birds fly.

Play One player is the leader and the others stand in a row in front of him. Alternatively, everyone sits around a table.

The leader starts by saying "My little bird is lively, is lively," and then goes on to name something followed by the word "fly" – for example, he might say "eggs fly."

If whatever he names can fly – for example, cockatoos – the players raise their arms and wave them about. If it cannot fly – as with eggs – the players should remain still.

A player who makes a mistake is out. The last player left in the game wins.

YES-NO BEANS

In Yes-no beans, players must guard against being tricked while at the same time trying to trick others.

Play Each player starts with five beans or any other unit of exchange.

The players circulate round the room, asking each

other question and replying to any questions that another player asks them. Players must not use the words yes or no in any of their replies.

Whenever a player succeeds in tricking another into saying yes or no, he gives that player one of his beans. The first player to get rid of all his beans wins the game.

LAUGHING HANDKERCHIEF

This game is often a riot of infectious laughter. It will be won only by a player who can start and stop laughing at will.

Play One player is the leader and stands in the center of a circle formed by the others.

The leader has a handkerchief which he drops as a signal for the other players to laugh. They must start laughing as soon as he lets go of the handkerchief and must stop when it touches the floor.

A player is out if he does not laugh the whole of the time that the handkerchief is falling or if he continues laughing after it has landed.

The last player left in the game wins and becomes the next leader.

SIMON SAYS

Simon says is an old party game that remains a great favorite.

Play One player is the leader and the others spread around the room in front of him.

The leader orders the others to make various actions – such as touching their toes or raising their arms. Whether or not they must obey his orders depends on how the orders are given.

If the leader begins the order with the words

"Simon says," the players must obey. If he does not begin with these words, they must not make the action. If a player makes a mistake he is out of the game. The leader encourages mistakes by:

(**a**) giving rapid orders;

(**b**) developing a rhythm with a repeated pattern of movements and then breaking it;

(**c**) making the actions himself for the others to follow.

The last person left in the game is the winner and becomes the next leader.

DO THIS, DO THAT!

This is played like Simon says except for the way in which the leader gives the orders. If the leader says "Do this!" the players should mimic his action. If he says "Do that!" they should remain still.

Do this, do that!

IN THE DITCH

This game is simpler than Simon says but calls for a lot of energy.

Play A line is marked along the floor with cushions or two parallel strands of yarn.

One player is the leader and the others space themselves out down one side of the line. One side is called "the bank" and the other side "the ditch". The leader orders the players to jump from side to side by calling out "In the ditch!" or "On the bank!" He can try to trick the players by calling the orders very quickly and repeating an order instead of alternating them.

A player must drop out if he makes a mistake. The winner is the last person left in the game.

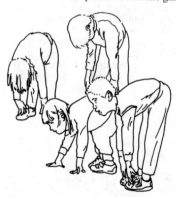

WHAT'S THE TIME, MR. WOLF?

Preparation One player chooses to be or is chosen as Mr. Wolf.

Play Mr. Wolf stands with his back to the others who advance one step at a time towards him from a reasonable distance. At each step, one member of the advancing group shouts "What's the time, Mr. Wolf?" The time is given by him and the group takes another step forward. At a moment of his own choosing Mr Wolf will, instead, shout the reply "Dinner Time!" He then turns rapidly and chases the others. The player who's caught becomes Mr. Wolf.

DEAD LIONS

Objective The player staying still the longest is the winning dead lion.

Preparation The organizer gets all the players to lie motionless on the ground or floor.

Play The organizer disqualifies every player who moves until only one dead lion is left lying. This last player is the winner. All disqualified players try to make the others move without actually touching them.

2. CHILDREN'S PARTY RACES

Individuals

Races of many different kinds are suitable for
indoor parties. Here we begin with a few ideas for
races in which individuals complete on their own
behalf rather than as members of a team. None of
these races requires any athletic ability!

NEWSPAPER WALK
Each player tries to be the first to walk the length
of the room on two sheets of newspaper.
Play Players stand in a line at one end of the room.
Each player is given two sheets of newspaper to
stand on, one sheet under each foot.
At the word "Go!" he starts to move across the
room on his newspaper. If he touches the floor with
any part of his body he must go back to the
beginning again.

TORTOISE RACE
Each player tries to be the last to finish.
Play Players line up along one side of the room.
At the word "Go!" they each start to move across
the room as slowly as possible. They must head
straight for the opposite wall.
A player is disqualified if he stops moving or
changes direction.

FISHERMEN
Each player tries to be the first to reel in his "fish".
Preparation Each player requires a fishing line
and fish – made by tying a teaspoon to a length of
strong thread wrapped around a spool.

Play Players stand in a line at one end of the room.
Each player is given a spoon and spool. He places
the spoon on the floor and then unwinds the thread
in a straight line to the other end of the room.
At the word "Go!" each player starts to wind in his
spoon by turning the spool, 'round and 'round in
his hands. He is not permitted to hold the thread in
one hand and wrap it around the spool.

RABBIT RACE

Each player tries to be the first to jerk his "rabbit"
along his piece of string.

Preparation One rabbit shape for each player is
cut out of cardboard. A small hole is made in its
center and a piece of string about 6ft. (1.8m.) long
threaded through the hole and tied to a chair.

Play Each player holds the free end of the piece of
string and moves the rabbit to that end. At the
work "Go!" each player, without touching his
rabbit, must jerk it along the string to the chair.

BOTTLE FISHING

Each player tries to be the first to ring his bottle.

Preparation Several bottles of the same size and
shape are needed, together with an equal number
of rings large enough to slip over the necks of the
bottles. Each ring should be tied to a length of
string.

Play Players sit or stand in a line, with a bottle in
front of each of them. Each player then tries to
"catch" his bottle, by getting his ring over his
bottle's neck.

Pairs

This group of party races is for people competing as one of a pair. Back to back race, Piggy back race and Three-legged race are all quite energetic and are best held in a large room.

BACK-TO-BACK RACE
Pairs of players try to be the first to run the course.
Play Players form pairs and line up at one end of the room.
Each pair of players stands back to back with their arms linked. At the word "Go!" the linked players race to the other end of the room. Pairs who become unlinked must go back to the beginning and start again.

PIGGY BACK RACE
This is another race in which pairs of players try to be the first to run a course.
Play Players form pairs and line up at one end of the room. One player from each pair gets on the other's back to be carried.
At the word "Go!" the pairs race to the other end of the room, where they must change places so that the carrier becomes the carried.
They must then race back to the original end of the room. If a player touches the floor while he is being carried, that pair must start again.

THREE-LEGGED RACE
Pairs of players try to be the first to run from one end of the room to the other.

Play Players form pairs and line up at one end of the room. A scarf is needed for each pair so that the right leg of one of the players in the pair can be tied to the left leg of his partner. At the word "Go!" pairs race to the other end of the room.

PATCHES
Players race to sew patches on their partners' clothes.

Preparation A square of material, a needle and thread are needed for each pair of players.

Play Each player finds a partner and one of them is given a square of material, a needle and a length of thread.

At the word "Go!" a player from each pair quickly sews his patch on his partner's clothes. (Big stitches are allowed!)

The first player to finish wins the heat. The other player in each pair then has a turn at sewing.

NECKLACE RACE
Each pair tries to be the first to thread all its beads.

Preparation 12 beads on a saucer, a needle and a length of thread are needed for each pair of players.

Play Players line up in pairs along one side of the room. Each saucer of beads is placed opposite a pair of players at the other end of the room. One player in each pair is given a needle and length of thread. At the word "Go!" each player with needle and thread must thread his needle and tie a large firm knot at one end of his thread. At the same time, his partner runs to the saucer, picks up two beads and returns with them.

When the first player in each pair has threaded his needle he takes the two beads from his partner and threads them while his partner goes back to the saucer for two more beads.

Play continues in the way until all 12 beads have been threaded. If any beads are dropped they must be picked up and threaded normally.

When a player has threaded all 12 beads, he removes the needle and ties the bead necklace around the partner's neck.

The game is won by the first pair to finish its necklace.

DUMB ARTISTS

Each pair tries to be the first to have one player recognize an animal drawn by the other. Players are not allowed to speak to each other.

Play Players form pairs, and partners stand opposite each other at different ends of the room. The players at one end are each given a pencil and a card with the name of an animal written on it. At the word "Go!" each of these players runs to his partner and, with the animal's name face down tries to draw the animal.

When his partner thinks that he recognizes the drawing, he takes the pencil and writes down the animal's name. If his answer is correct, his partner nods his head and both players run to the other end of the room.

If the answer is incorrect, his partner shakes his head, takes the pencil back and continues drawing. The game is won by the first pair to reach the other end of the room after the animal has been guessed.

Teams

There is a fantastic variety of party races for
competitors divided into two or more teams. Some
races are organized on a relay basis, with each
team member in turn being required to perform a
particular activity. Other races involve individual
team member competing separately for points.

NUMBER PARADE
Objective Each team tries to be the first to parade
a number called by the organizer.
Preparation Single digits from zero to nine are
drawn on separate pieces of card. The digits should
be about 3in. (8cm.) high. There may be either one
or two cards for each player but there should be
the same set of digits for each team.
In addition, a list of numbers using the digits
available to each team is drawn up.
Play The teams form lines and each player is given
either one or two of the cards.
The organizer calls out a number – for example, he
might call "469."
Immediately, the players in each team with the
digits 4, 6 and 9 rush to the front and line up
holding their digits so that they read "469."
The first team to parade the number correctly
scores a point.
Players return to their teams and another number
is called.
To make the game more interesting, the organizer

can set easy sums for the players to solve and parade.

WORD PARADE

This is played like Number parade except that letters are written on the cards and words are called out to be spelled and paraded by the players.

MYSTERY NUMBERS

Objective Each team's players try to be fastest at solving clues and running around their teams.

Preparation It is a good idea to prepare a list of clues indicating particular numbers. If there are seven players in a team, clues for numbers one through seven will be needed. For example, for number six the clues might be: half a dozen, a hexagon, an insect's legs, June, the sides of a cube.

Play Players line up behind their leaders and sit down. In each team, players are numbered off starting with the leader as number one.

The organizer calls out a clue. As soon as a player recognizes that it refers to his number, he jumps up, runs around his team and sits down in his place again.

The first player back scores a point for his team. When all the players are seated again, the organizer calls out another clue.

End The team with the most points at the end of a time limit wins the game.

SIMPLE NUMBERS

This is played in the same way as Mystery numbers except that the numbers are not hidden in clues. The organizer simply calls out each number.

LADDERS

Ladders can be played like either Mystery numbers or Simple numbers (p.61). The difference is that the teams sit in two rows facing each other. It is recommended that players take off their shoes for this game. Each player sits with his legs outstretched and his feet touching those of the opposing player with the same number as himself. When a player's number is called or indicated he runs up between the lines over the other players' legs, back down behind his team and then up between the lines to return to his place.

MY MOTHERS CAKE

This is played in the same way as Ladders except that players are given the name of an ingredient instead of a number.

The organizer then tells a story about how the cake was made and while telling it he mentions all the various ingredients. When a player hears the name of the ingredient he must race around as in Ladders.

YARN TANGLES

Teams of four players try to be first to untangle balls of yarn wrapped around chairs.

Preparation A chair and four different colored balls of yarn are needed for each team.

Play Players form into teams of four. Each team is given four balls of yarn and a chair.

Teams are then allowed about one minute in which to tangle their yarn around their chairs. They are not allowed to lift up their chairs or to make deliberate knots in the yarn.

At the end of the time limit, the organizer calls

"Stop!" and teams must move around to a different chair.

At the word "Go!" teams start to disentangle the yarn from their new chair. Each player winds one of the balls of yarn. Players are not allowed to pick up the chair or deliberately break the yarn.

The game is won by the first team to untangle the yarn into four separate balls.

CROCODILE RACE

This is an amusing race for teams of players.

Play Players divide into teams and line up behind their leaders at one end of the room. Players then squat on their heels, each with his hands on the shoulders or waist of the player in front of him.

At the word "Go!" the "crocodiles" move forward by little jumps or bounces. If a player loses contact with the player in front of him, his team must stop and reassemble. For reassembling, the hind end of the crocodile must stay where it is while the front end moves back to join it.

The first team to reach the other end of the room intact wins the race.

FLYING FISH

Objective In the game (also known as Kippers) teams race each other at fanning "fish" across the room.

Preparation A "fish" about 10in. (25cm.) long is made for each player out of thick paper – the plumper the fish, the better it will "fly." Each team is given a folded newspaper or magazine.

Play Players line up behind their leaders at one end of the room. A plate is placed on the floor at

the other end of the room opposite each team.
At the word "Go!" each leader places his fish on
the floor and fans it with the newspaper, down the
room and onto the plate.
As soon as he has done this, he races back to his
team and hands the newspaper to the next player
in line.
Each player in turns fans his fish across the room
and onto the plate, and the first team to finish wins
the game.

BURST THE BAG

Objective Teams race each other to be the first to
blow up and burst paper bags.

Play Players line up behind their leaders. Paper
bags, one for each player, are placed on chairs
opposite each team leader. At the word "Go!" each
leader runs to the chair, takes a paper bag, blows it
up and bursts it with his hands.
As soon as he has done this, he runs back to his
team and touches the next player. As soon as this
player is touched, he takes his turn at bursting a
bag.
Play continues in this way until each player has
burst a bag – the first team to finish being the
winners.

SURPRISE SENTENCES

Objective Each team tries to write a sentence,
with each player in the team writing one word of it.

Preparation For each team, a large sheet of paper
is attached to a wall or to a board propped upright.

Play Each team lines up opposite its sheet of
paper and the leader is given a pencil.

At the word "Go!" he runs up to his paper and writes any word he likes. He then runs back to his team, hands the pencil to the next player and goes to the end of his team.

As soon as the next player gets the pencil, he goes to the paper and adds a second word either in front of, or behind, the leader's word.

Play continues in this way with each player adding one word. The words should be chosen and put together so that they can be part of a grammatically correct sentence.

Each player, except the last, must avoid completing the sentence. The last player should be able to complete the sentence by adding just one word and he also puts in the punctuation.

Players may not confer and choose a sentence before writing their words.

End The first team to construct a sentence with one word from each player wins the game.

NOSE IN THE MATCHBOX

Play Players divide into teams and line up beside their leaders. A matchbox lid is given to each leader.

On the word "Go!" he lodges it on his nose and passes it onto the next player's nose without using his hands.

In this way, the matchbox lid is passed down the line. If a player touches the lid with his hands or drops it, it is returned to the leader to start again.

End The first team to succeed in passing the matchbox lid down the line wins.

DOUBLE PASS

Objective Players in each team try to pass objects behind them and in front of them in two directions.

Preparation Two identical piles of objects are collected, one of each team. Alternatively, a deck of cards may be divided between the teams.

Play Players divide into teams and sit in a line to the left of their leaders. One pile of objects, or cards, is placed beside the leader.

On the word "Go!" he starts passing the objects, one after the other, down the line.

Only right hands are used until the object reaches the end of the line. Then only left hands are used to return the objects behind the players' backs.

As objects arrive back at the beginning again, the leader makes a pile of the returned objects.

End The first team to return all the objects wins.

SWITCHBACK

Objective Each team tries to be quickest at passing through a hoop.

Play Players divide into teams and line up behind their leader. A hoop is given to each leader.

On the word "Go!" the leader puts the hoop over his head, drops it to the ground, and steps out of it. The next player steps into the hoop, lifts it over his head and hands it to the next player.

The hoop is passed down the line in this way, players putting the hoop over their heads and stepping into it alternately.

When the last player has passed through the hoop, he runs with it to the front of the line and passes it back as before. This continues with each player taking a turn at the head of the line.

End The first team with its leader at the front again wins.

HAT AND SCARF

Objective Players of each team try to be the quickest at dressing up and running around the team.

Preparation A hat, a scarf, a coat and a pair of gloves are collected for each team.

Play Teams line up behind their leaders and a set of clothes is placed on a chair in front of each team. At the word "Go!" each leader runs to the chair, puts on the clothes, and runs around his team. He then takes off the clothes and gives them to the next player to dress up in

Play continues in this way down the line. When the last player has run around his team, he places the clothes on the chair.

End The first team with its set of clothes back on the chair wins the game.

EMPTYING SOCKS

Objective Each team tries to be the first to remove a variety of objects in their correct order from a long sock.

Preparation Identical groups of small objects are put into long socks, one sock for each team. There should be only one item of each kind in each group. The objects might be buttons, beans, coins of different sizes, hairpins, pebbles, etc.

Play Teams line up opposite their leaders. Each leader is given a sock to hold. The organizer announces the first object to be found.

Immediately the first player in each team runs to his leader and puts his hand in the sock. He feels for the object and picks it out of the sock. If he makes a mistake, he returns the object and tries again.

If he takes out the correct object he gives it to the organizer and is told the next object to be retrieved. He returns to his team, tells the next player what to search for and stands at the back of his team.

As soon as the next player knows what to find, he takes his turn at feeling for an object in the sock. Play continues in this way until each object has been retrieved and the first team to finish wins.

FRUIT COLORS

Objective Each team tries to be the first to color in pictures of fruit.

Preparation For each team, outlines of fruit (one per player) are drawn on a large sheet of paper. The drawings should be the same for each team. The paper is attached to a wall or laid out on a table.

Play Teams line up behind their leaders at the opposite end of the room to the drawings. Each leader is given a box of crayons.

At the word "Go!" he runs to his team's sheet of paper and colors in one of the pieces of fruit. He then goes back to his team, hands the box of crayons to the next player and stands at the back of his team.

As soon as the second player gets the crayons, he goes and colors in another fruit; and so on, down the line of players. If a crayon is dropped on the floor, the player with the box must pick it up.

End The first team to color in all its fruit wins.

BALLOON PASS

Objective Each team tries to be quickest at passing a balloon overhead.

Play Players divide into teams and form lines behind their leaders. Each leader is given a balloon. On the word "Go!" he passes it over his head to the player behind him. This player in turn passes the balloon back over his head. In this way the balloon is passed down the entire line. When the last player gets the balloon, he runs to the front of his line and passes the balloon back in the same way as before. Thus each player takes a turn at the head of the line.

End The winning team is the first one to have its leader at the front of the line again.

TUNNEL BALL

This is played like balloon pass except that players stand with their legs apart and pass the balloon back between their legs.

BALLOON HOP

Objective Teams try to be the first to find and inflate all the balloons belonging to them.

Preparation Balloons of as many different colors as there are teams should be bought, and each, and each player in each team will need a balloon.

Play Players line up behind their leaders. Each team is assigned a color. The balloons are placed in a pile at the end of the room.

At the word "Go!" each leader hops across the room, finds a balloon of his team's color and hops back with it to his team. When he returns, the next player hops across the room to find a balloon; and so on, until each player has a balloon.

When players return to their teams, they inflate the balloons and fasten the necks. If a player has a lot of difficulty tying his balloon, another player in his team may help him.

End The first team with all its balloons blown up and tied wins.

EGG CUPS

Objective Each player tries to blow a ping pong ball from one egg cup to another.

Play Players divide into teams and line up beside their leaders. Two egg cups and a ping pong ball are given to each leader. At the word "Go!" the leader blows the ping pong ball from one egg cup to the other. He may hold the egg cups so that they touch, but he may not merely tip the ball from one cup to the other.

As soon as the leader has finished, he hands the cups and the ping pong ball to the next player; and so on, down the line, until each player has blown the ball from one egg cup to the other.

If the ball falls from the egg cups, or is handled or tipped instead of blown, it is returned to the leader who must start again.

End The first team whose players have blown the ping pong ball from one cup to the other wins.

HURRY WAITER!

Objective Players try to keep a ping pong ball balanced on a plate while weaving in and out of a line of their teammates.

Play Players divide into teams and stand in a line behind their leaders. Each leader is given a ping pong ball on a plate.

At the word "Go!" he weaves in and out between the players in his team as quickly as he can without dropping the ping pong ball.

When he reaches the end of the line, he runs straight to the head of the line again and hands the plate and ball to the next player, saying "Here is your breakfast, Sir (or Madam)" as he does so.

This procedure is repeated, with each player beginning at the head of the line and returning to his place as soon as he has handed the "breakfast" to the next player in turn.

If a player drops the ball, he must go back to the head of the line and start again. The first team to finish wins the game.

PASSING THE ORANGE

Objective Seated players try to pass an orange down the line using their feet, or (in an alternative version) by using their chins!

Play Players divide into teams and sit in a line on the floor beside their leaders. Each leader is given an orange and, legs together, cradles it on his feet. On the word "Go!" he passes the orange to the feet of the next player.

(Alternatively, the leader tucks the orange under his chin. The next player takes the orange from him, also using his chin – neither player may use his hands.) Using either one of these ways, the orange is passed from player to player. If the orange drops on the floor, or if a player uses his hands, the orange is returned to the leader to start again.

End The first team to pass the orange down the line wins.

Pencil and paper games

Pencil and paper games need only the simplest equipment, yet they can provide a great scope for the imagination, increase a player's general knowledge and – above all – be a highly enjoyable way of passing time. Pencil and paper games fall basically into two categories: word games and games in which pictures or symbols are drawn.

KEYWORD

Keyword, sometimes called Hidden words, can be played by any number of people.

The players choose a "keyword" containing at least seven letters. Each player then tries to make as many words as possible from the letters in the keyword. The letter may be used in any order, but a letter may be used in any one word only as many times as it appears in the keyword.

Generally, proper nouns (capitalized words) or words with fewer than four letters are not allowed; nor are abbreviations or plurals.

The game may be played just for interest, with players working together; or it may be made into a contest, with individuals competing to find most words in an agreed length of time.

CROSSWORDS

This intriguing game can be adapted for play by any number of people. If up to five are playing, each of them draws a square divided into five squares by five on a piece of paper. If more people take part, or if players wish to lengthen the game, the number of squares can be increased to, say, seven by seven.

Each of the players in turn calls out any letter of the alphabet. As each letter is called, all players write it into any square of their choice, with the objective of forming words of two or more letters reading either across or down.

Generally, abbreviations or proper nouns (names, etc.) may not be used. Once a letter has been written down, it cannot be moved to another square. Players continue to call out letters until all the individual squares have been filled.

The number of points scored is equal to the number of letters in each word (one-letter words do not count). Thus a three-letter word scores three points. If a word fills an entire row or column, one bonus point is scored in addition to the score for that word. No ending of a word can form the beginning of another word in the same row or column. For example, if a row contains the letters "i, f, e, n, d" the player may score four points for the word "fend" but cannot, in addition, score two points for the word "if."

Each player adds together each of his horizontal and vertical totals; the winning player is the one with the highest score (see page 74).

Crosswords

Acrostics

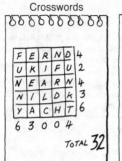

ACROSTICS

Acrostics is a popular word-building game. A word of at least three letters is chosen.

Each player writes the word in a column down the left-hand side of a piece of paper; he then writes the same word, but with the letters reversed, down the right-hand side of the page.

The player fills in the space between the two columns with the same number of words as there are letters in the keyword – and starting and ending each word with the letter at either side. For example, if the keyword is "stem" a player's words might read: scream, trundle, earliest, manageress. The winner could be either the first person to fill in all the words, or the player with the longest or most original words.

CATEGORIES

One of the best-known pencil and paper games, Categories can be played at either a simple or a sophisticated level.

Preparation Each player (there may be any number) is given a pencil and a piece of paper. The players decide on between six and a dozen different categories; these may be easy ones for children (e.g. girls' or boys' names, animals, colors) or more difficult for adults (e.g. politicians, rivers, chemicals). Each player lists the categories on his piece of paper.

One of the players chooses any letter of the alphabet – preferably an "easy" letter such as "a" or "d" if children are playing. Experienced players can make the game more challenging by choosing more difficult letters such as "j" or "k".

Players may decide to play to an agreed time limit of, say, 15 minutes.

Play The players try to find a word beginning with the chosen letter for each of the categories (e.g. if the chosen letter is "p" all the words must begin with that letter). They write down their words next to the appropriate category, trying where possible to think of words that none of the other players will have chosen.

Scoring Writing must stop as soon as the time limit is up, or as soon as one player has finished. Each player in turn then reads out his list of words. If he has found a word not thought of by any other player, he scores two points for that word. If, however, one or more of the other players has also chosen the same word, each of them scores only one point. If the player could not find a word at all, or if his choice of word did not correctly fit the category, he gets no points. (Any disagreement about the relevance of a word to a category must be resolved by a vote among the other players.) The winner is the player with the highest score for his list of words.

Subsequent rounds Any number of rounds may be played, using either the same or different

CATEGORIES	P.	S.
Color	Pink	Scarlet
Boy's name	Paul	Stephan
City	Paris	Sydney
Country	Portugal	Spain
Island	Pitcairn	Seychelles
Mountain	Pilatus	Stromboli
Composer	Paderewski	Scarlatti

CATEGORIES	G.	A.	M.	E.
Color	Green	Amber	Magenta	Emerald
Boy's name	George	Andrew	Martin	Ernest
City	Glasgow	Amsterdam	Mombassa	Essen
Country	Greece	Austria	Morocco	England
Island	Galapagos	Arran	Malta	Ellis
Composer	Grieg	Albinoni	Mozart	Elgar
Girl's name	Glenda	Anne	Mary	Edna

categories; the chosen letter, however, must be different for each round. Players may take turns to choose a letter at the start of a round. Players make a note of their scores at the end of each round. The winner is the player with the highest points total at the end of the final round.

GUGGENHEIM

Guggenheim is a slightly more complicated version of Categories. Instead of choosing only one letter for each round of play, the players choose a keyword of about four or five letters.

The letters of the keyword are written spaced out to the right of the list of categories, and players try to find words for each of the categories beginning with the letter heading each column.

TRANSFORMATION

Two words with the same number of letters are chosen. Each player writes down the two words. He tries to change the first word into the second word by altering only one letter at a time and each time forming a new word.

For example, "dog" could be changed to "cat" in four words as follows: dog, cog, cot, cat. It is easiest to begin with three- or four-letter words until the players are quite practiced – when five or even six letter words may be tried.

The winner is the player who completes the changes using the fewest number of words.

ANAGRAMS

This game is also called Jumbled words. Any number of players may take part. One of them prepares a list of words belonging to a particular category (e.g. flowers, cities, poets) and jumbles up the letter in each word.

Each of the other players is given a list of the jumbled words and their category, and tries to rearrange the letters back into the original words. For example, " peilmidhun" should be "delphinium" and "wodronsp" should be "snowdrop."

The first player to rearrange all the words correctly, or the player with most correct words after a given time, wins the game.

More experienced players may like to make up anagrams of their own by rearranging the letters in a word to make one or more other words (e.g. "angered" is an anagram of "derange").

SYNONYMS

A list of 10 to 20 words is prepared, and a copy given to each player. The objective is to find a synonym (word with the same meaning) for each word on the list. If a player can think of more than one synonym for any word he should write down the shortest one.

After an agreed length of time, the players' lists are checked.

The winner is the player who finds a synonym for the most words, or, if two or more players have an equal number of synonyms, the player with the lowest total of letters in his synonyms.

FILL INS

A list of 30 to 40 words is prepared and kept hidden from the players.

Each player is then given the first and last letters

and the number of letters missing from each word on the list. The winner is the first player to fill in all the blanks correctly. Alternatively, the players may be allowed an agreed length of time and then the winner is the player with the most correct words.

TELEGRAMS

Players are given or make up a list of 15 letters and must use each of them – in the order given – as the initial letter of a word in a 15-word telegram. (Alternatively, the players are given or select a word of about 10-15 letters, e.g. blackberries, so that the first word must begin with "b", the second with "l", and so on.)

The telegram may include one or two place names and may – if the player wishes – have the name of the "sender" as the last word. Stops (or periods) may be used for punctuation. The winner is the first player to complete his telegram, or, if a time limit has been set, the player whose telegram is judged to be the best at the end of the time set.

Telegrams

BLACKBERRIES

BRING LAMP AND CHISEL STOP KNOW BEST ENTRY ROUTE STOP REST IS EASY STOP SID

CONSEQUENCES

Consequences is a favourite among children and is a game purely to be enjoyed – there are no winners or losers. Any number of players can take part, and each of them is provided with a piece of paper and pencil.

The objective is to write as many stories as there are participants, with each person contributing to each of the stories.

Play One person is chosen as "caller" (this does not exclude him from taking part). He calls out the first part of the story. Each person writes down an appropriate name, phrase, or sentence, making it as humorous as possible. He then folds over the top of the piece of paper to hide what he has written, and passes the paper to the player to his left. The caller then says the next part of the story, and the players write something on the paper they have just received from their neighbors.

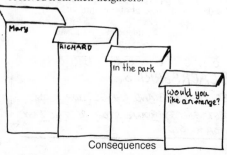

Consequences

This procedure is repeated until the story is complete. Any theme may be used, but the one described here is perhaps the best know.

(1) "A girl..." (players write the name of someone known to them, or alternatively a famous personality or fictional character);
(2) "met a boy..." (again, the players may choose any name of their choice);
(3) "at...beside...in..." (the player may choose any location);
(4) "he said...";
(5) "she said...";
(6) "the consequence was...";
(7) "and the world said..."

When the story is complete, each player passes the pieces of paper on which he wrote the last sentence to the person to his left. The pieces of paper are unfolded and the stories read out one by one – they may not be fictional masterpieces but are sure to provide a lot of fun!

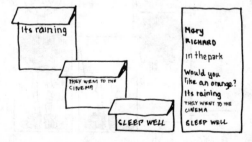

PICTURE CONSEQUENCES

This game has similarities with standard
Consequences, but instead of writing words, the
players draw parts of an animal or a person dressed
in funny clothing – starting with the head and
finishing with the feet.

When the sheets of paper are folded over, a part of
the last drawing is left showing, so as to give a hint
to the next player.

For example, after drawing the head, the paper
should be folded so that the edges of the neck are
showing.

After drawing the feet, players may write down the
name of the person whom they want the figure to
represent!

Picture consequences

HANGMAN

Hangman is a popular game for two or more players. One person thinks of a word of about five or six letters. He writes down the same number of dashes as there are letters in his word.

The other players may then start guessing the letters in the word, calling out one letter at a time. If the guess is a successful one, the letter is written by the first player about the appropriate dash – if it appears more than once in a word it must be entered as often as it occurs.

If the guess is an incorrect one, however, the first player may start to draw a hanged man – one line of the drawing representing each wrong letter.

The other players must try to guess the secret word before the first player can complete the drawing of the hanged man.

If one player guesses the word (this should become easier as the game progresses) he may take a turn at choosing a word. If the hanged man is completed before the word is guessed the same player may choose another word.

To make the game more difficult, longer words may be chosen. Alternatively, the player may choose a group of words making a proverb or the title of a book or film – and should give the other players a clue as to the category.

A typical sequence is over the page.

Hangman

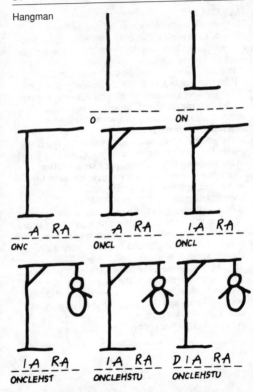

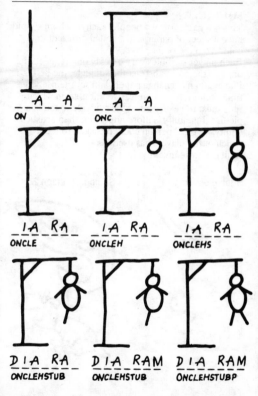

SQUIGGLES

This is a game for two people, each of whom should have a sheet of paper, and a pencil different in color from the other player's.

Each player scribbles very quickly on his sheet of paper – the more abstract the squiggle, the better. Players then exchange papers and set themselves a time limit of, for example, two minutes, in which they must use every bit of the squiggle to make a picture. Ingenuity is more important than artistic ability – a third person could be asked to judge which of the players has used his squiggle more inventively.

Squiggles: stage 1   Squiggles: stage 2

TIC TAC TOE

A favorite for generations, this game for two people is sometimes over in a matter of seconds! Two vertical lines are drawn with two horizontal lines crossing them, forming nine spaces. Players decide which of them is to draw circles and which of them crosses.

Taking turns, the players make their mark in any vacant space until one of them manages to get three of his marks in a row (either horizontally, vertically or diagonally.)

He then draws a line through his winning row and the game comes to an end.

If neither player succeeds in forming a row, the game is considered drawn.

As the player who draws first has a better chance of winning, players usually swop their starting order after each game.

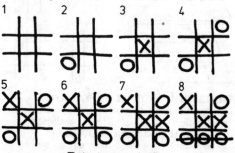

Tic tac toe: sample play

Three-dimensional Tic tac toe

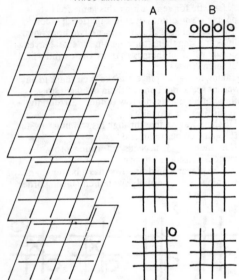

THREE-DIMENSIONAL TIC TAC TOE
Based on the standard game, the three-dimensional
version offers a lengthier and more challenging
alternative. Three-dimensional Tic tac toe
can be bought as a game, but can equally well be
played with pencil and paper.

A vertical; B and C horizontal; D, E and F diagonal.

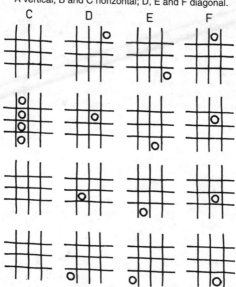

The cube may be represented diagrammatically by 64 squares – as shown. For actual play, each "layer" of the cube is drawn out individually.

Playing procedure is similar to standard Tic tac toe, but the winner is the first player to get four of his marks in a row. (Illustrations show winning rows.)

Boxes

This is a simple but amusing game for two players. Any number of dots is drawn on a sheet of paper – the dots are drawn in rows to form a square. Ten rows by ten is a good number.

Players take alternate turns. In each turn they may draw horizontal or vertical line to join up and two dots that are next to each other.

The objective is to complete (with a fourth line) as many squares or "boxes" as possible. Whenever a

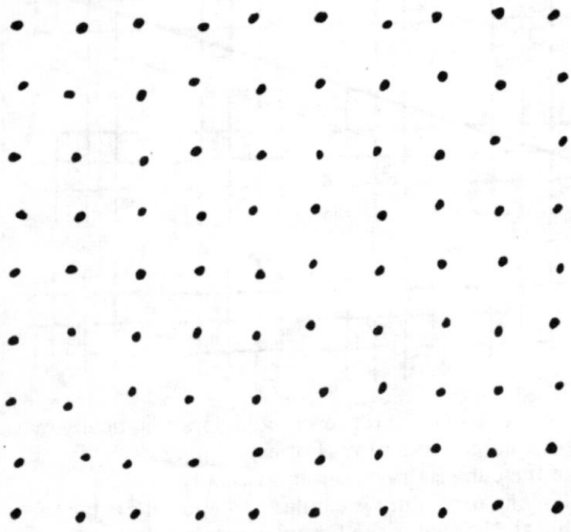

Boxes: sample play

player completes a box he initials it and may draw
another line that does not complete a box.

As soon as there are no more dots to be joined – all
the boxes having been filled – the game ends. The
player with the highest number of initialed boxes is
the winner.

Another way of playing is to try to form the lowest
number of boxes – the players join up as many dots
as they can before being forced to complete a box.
The winner is the player with the fewest initialed
boxes.

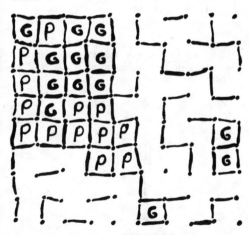

SPROUTS

Sprouts has certain similarities with Boxes, but needs rather more ingenuity to win!

Two players take part. About six or so dots are drawn – well spaced-out – on a piece of paper (more may be drawn for a longer game.)

Taking turns, each player draws a line joining any two dots or joining a dot to itself. He then draws a dot anywhere along the line he has just made, and his turn ends. When drawing a line, the following rules must be observed:

(**a**) no line may cross itself;

(**b**) no line may cross a line that has already been drawn;

(**c**) no line may be drawn through a dot;

(**d**) a dot may have no more than three lines leaving it.

The last person able to draw a legal line is the winner.

Disallowed sprouts

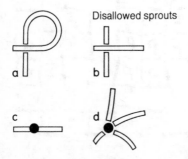

a

b

c

d

PICTURES

Pictures is best played by two teams of at least three players each. In addition, there must be an organizer who belongs to neither team.

The organizer makes a list of half a dozen or so book titles, proverbs or other subjects (they need not be in the same category).

The organizer whispers the first title on the list to on player from each team. This player returns to his team (the team should preferably be in separate rooms) and must draw a picture representing the title. He may add to his drawing or make further drawings – until one of his teammates has correctly guessed the answer. (No verbal clues may be given, however!)

As soon as one player has guessed the title, he may go to the organizer for the next title on the list. The winning team is the first one to guess all the titles on the organizer's list.

BATTLESHIPS

This is an extremely popular game for two players, each of whom needs a pencil and piece of graph paper.

The players should sit so that they cannot see the other's paper.

Each or them draws two identical playing areas, ten squares by ten squares in size.

In order to identify each square, the playing areas have numbers down one side and letters across the top (so the top left-hand square is A1; the bottom left-hand square is A10, etc.).

Each player marks one playing area his "home fleet" and the other playing area the "enemy fleet."

Each player has his own fleet of ships that he may position anywhere within his home fleet area.

His fleet comprises:

(**a**) one battleship, four squares long;

(**b**) two cruisers, each three squares long;

(**c**) three destroyers, each two squares long; and

(**d**) four submarines, each one square only.

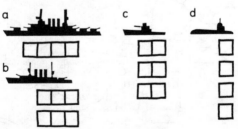

See over for opponent's (enemy) fleet positions.

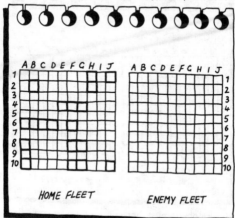

HOME FLEET   ENEMY FLEET

He "positions" his ships by outlining the
appropriate number of squares.
The squares representing each ship must be in a
row, either across or down. There must also be at
least one vacant square between ships.
The players' objective is to destroy their opponent's
entire fleet by a series of "hits." Players take
alternate turns. In each turn, a player may attempt
three hits: he calls out the names of any three
squares – marking them on his enemy fleet area as
he does so.

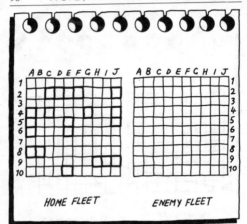

His opponent must then consult his own home fleet
area to see whether any of these squares are
occupied. If they are, he must state how many and
the category of ship hit.

In order to sink a ship, every one of its component
squares must have received a hit. The game
continues with both players marking the state of
their own and the enemy's fleet – this may be done
by shading or outlining squares, or in some other
chosen manner.

There is no limit to the number of hits each player
may attempt – the game comes to an end as soon as
one player destroys his opponent's fleet.

BURIED TREASURE

This is a much simpler version of Battleships (p.94) and is particularly suitable for young children. It is a game for two, with a third person needed to help at the beginning of the game.

Each player draws an area nine squares by seven and marks it in the same manner as the Battleships, so that each square has a name.

The third person designates any four of the letters from A to I to one player, and any four of the remaining letters to the other player; he then does the same thing with three of the numbers from 1 to 7. Neither player knows which letters and numbers have been designated to his opponent, nor which letter and number are left over – this is the square in which the treasure is "buried" and which the players must try to identify.

Players take turns to ask each other whether they hold a particular letter or number. Although a respondent must always give a truthful answer, a player may – if he wishes – enquire about a letter or number that he holds himself, so as to mislead. The first player to locate the treasure by this mixture of bluff and elimination wins the game.

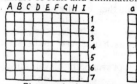

Players, designated letters and numbers

CRYSTALS

In this sophisticated pattern visualizing game, each player tries to form symmetrical shapes known as "crystals."

Equipment All that is needed is a sheet of graph paper and as many differently colored crayons as there are players.

The number of squares used for each game depends on the number of players: if two take part (the best number) about 20 rows of 20 squares each would for a suitable area.

Objective Each player attempts to "grow" crystals on the paper with the aim of filling more squares than his opponent.

A player does not score points for the number of crystals he grows, but for the number of squares his crystals cover.

A crystal is made up of "atoms," each of which occupies a single square. In growing crystals, players must observe certain rules of symmetry that determine whether or not a crystal is legal. The symmetry of a crystal can be determined by visualizing four axes through its center: horizontal, vertical, and two diagonal axes. Once the axes have been "drawn," it should theoretically be possible to fold the crystal along each of the four axes to produce corresponding "mirror" halves that, when folded, exactly overlay each other (i.e. are the same shape and size).

In addition to the rules of symmetry, players must observe the following:

(a) a legitimate crystal may be formed from four or

Examples of allowed "crystals"

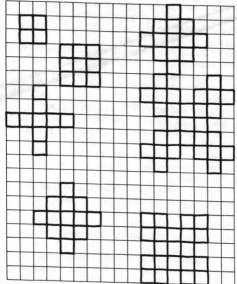

more atoms drawn by one player only;
(b) the atoms forming a crystal must be joined along their sides – they may not be connected only by their corners;
(c) a crystal may not contain any empty atoms (i.e. holes).

Play Players decide on their playing order and each one in turn shades in any one square of his choice – each player using a crayon of a different color.

In the first few turns, players rarely try to grow a crystal.

Instead, they place single atoms around the playing area in order to establish potential crystal sites. As play progesses, players will see which atoms are best placed for growing crystals and add to them as appropriate.

When a player thinks he has grown a crystal, he declares it, and rings the area that it covers.

A player with a winning advantage will try to retain the lead by either blocking his opponents' attempts at growing crystals, or by growing long narrow crystals that – although not high scoring – restrict the playing area.

Play ends when no blank squares are left, or when the players agree that no more crystals can be formed.

Scoring Players work out which of the crystals are legal, and count the number of squares each crystal covers.

Any crystal that does not demonstrate symmetry around each of the four axes is not legal and does not score.

The number of squares in the legal crystals that each player has grown are added up, and the player with most squares wins the game.

AGGRESSION

Aggression is a game in which players fight imaginary battles in a bid to occupy the maximum amount of territory.

Two players are ideal – though the game can also be played by three or more, who may choose to form teams. Each player must have a crayon of a different color.

Playing area A large piece of paper is used. One player begins by drawing the boundaries of an imaginary country; each player in turn then draws the outline of an imaginary country.

Any number of countries may be drawn (20 is an average number if two play) and they can be any shape or color.

When the agreed number of countries has been drawn, each is clearly marked with a different letter of the alphabet (see p.102).

Armies Each player is allotted 100 armies. Taking turns with his opponent, he chooses a country that he intends to occupy and writes within it how many armies he is allocating to it.

(Once a country has been occupied, no player may add further armies to it.)

This procedure continues until all the countries have been occupied, or until each player has allocated all his armies.

Play The player who chose the first country has the opening move. His objective is to retain more occupied countries than his opponent; to achieve this he "attacks" enemy armies in adjacent countries. (Adjacent countries are defined as those with a common boundary.) A player may attack with armies from more than one country – provided

Drawing the boundaries

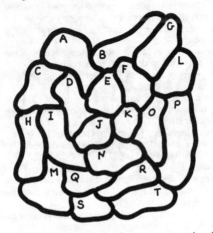

they are all in countries that have a common border
with the country under attack.
If the number of armies located in the attacking
country or countries is greater than those located in
the defending country, the defending army is
conquered – its armies are crossed off and can take
no further part in the game. (The armies used to
conquer a country may be reused.)
Players take it in turns to conquer countries until
one or both of them cannot mount any further
attacks.

Positioning the armies

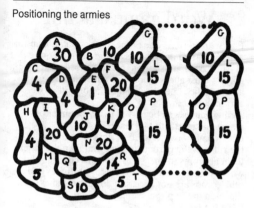

Conquering
L conquers G but is then
conquered by OP

Scoring At the end of the game the players total
the number of countries each of them retains. The
winner is the player with the highest number of
unconquered countries – he need not necessarily be
the player who made the greatest number of
conquests.

Word games: acting

Play with words is one of the most popular forms of amusement. Games in this first group all require players to act, most often in mime, words that other players must guess. There is no need for any great acting ability, but a lively imagination will prove extremely useful!

Acting games can be played by any number of players divided into two teams.

One team chooses a word or phrase according to the rules of the particular game and then the other team attempts to guess it. The teams change roles whenever a correct guess is made. Costumes and other props are not necessary for these games, but they add to the players' enjoyment.

CHARADES

Charades is probably the best known and most popular of all word games involving acting.

The objective is for one team to guess a word with several syllables that is acted out in mime by the other team.

Play The acting team leaves the room and decides on a suitable word. Usually words of three syllables are chosen, but players may choose words of only two syllables or of four or more.

This word is then presented to the other team in mime scenes representing the different syllables, and then in a final scene representing the whole word.

Usually there is one scene for each syllable,

although players may choose to represent two syllables in a single scene. (For example, the word "decorate" could be broken down as "deck-or-rate" or as "decor-ate.") One of the actors must announce the number of scenes before miming begins. The actors usually leave the room between scenes and the guessing team is then free to discuss its ideas. It is advisable for players to agree on a time limit for guessing words after the final scene.

An example of the sort of word that might be chosen is "nightingale" which was used in a charade scene in the book *Vanity Fair* by the nineteenth-century English novelist, William Thackeray. Nightingale breaks down into three syllables and could be represented by:

(a) a "night" scene with people going to bed or sleeping.

(b) an "inn" scene with people drinking and enjoying themselves;

(c) a "gale" scene with people being blown down a street;

(d) a "nightingale" scene with people flapping their arms and imitating bird song.

CATEGORY CHARADES

This game is played in the same way as standard Charades except that the teams must choose words that belong to a previously agreed category and there is no miming of the full word.

Ideas for categories are;

(a) towns (e.g. "cam-bridge," "prince-ton");

(b) people's names (e.g. "rob-in," "car-row-line");

(c) animals (e.g. "lie-on," "buff-a-low");

(d) flowers (e.g. "snow-drop," "butter-cup").

PROVERB CHARADES

Proverb charades is played in the same way as standard Charades except that teams choose a proverb or well-known quotation, which they then act out word by word or in groups of several words. A good proverb for this game would be "a bird in the hand is worth two in the bush."

SPOKEN CHARADES

This game is played in the same way as standard Charades except that the actors speak. Instead of miming scenes representing the syllables and then the full word, the players must mention them while acting in the different scenes. This game is easier to play than most Charades games, and for this reason is particularly popular with younger children.

DUMB CRAMBO

Dumb crambo is a very old game of the Charades family. It was particularly popular in the nineteenth century.

Objective After receiving a rhyming clue, a team attempts to guess and mime a word, usually a verb chosen by the opposing team.

Play the first team chooses a word, for example "feel" and then tells the second team a word rhyming with it, for example "steal."

It is obviously best for this game to choose a word that has several words rhyming with it. For example, other words that rhyme with "feel" are "heal," "keel," "reel," "deal," and "peel."

The second team then attempts to guess the chosen word and must mime its guesses. A maximum of three guesses is allowed. If a guess is incorrect, members of the other team hiss or boo; if a guess is correct they clap their hands.

A team scores one point each time it guesses a word. Teams change roles after a word is guessed or after three incorrect guesses. The game is won by the team with most points when play ends.

IN THE MANNER OF THE WORD

This is an amusing acting game in which players attempt to guess adverbs.

Play One player chooses an adverb, such as rapidly, quietly or amusingly. The other players, in turn then ask him to carry out some action "in the manner of the word." For example a player might say; "eat in the manner of the word," "walk in the manner of the word," or "laugh in the manner of the word."

The player who chooses the adverb must do as the other players ask, and the other players may make guesses as soon as acting begins.

The first player to guess an adverb correctly scores one point. If no one guesses the word after each of the players has asked for an action, the player who chose the adverb receives one point.

The game is won by the player with most points after each of the players has had a turn at choosing the adverb.

Word games: guessing

Games in this group of word games require players to identify what another player is thinking. Many of them can be made either easy or difficult to suit the ages and abilities of the people taking part.

I-SPY

I-spy is an excellent game for children learning to spell. It is also fun for older children, who can try to outwit each other by "spying" inconspicuous objects.

Objective Each players tries to be the first to guess which visible object one of them has spied.

Play Two or more people can play, and one of them is chosen to start. He says, "I spy, with my little eye something beginning with..." and gives the first letter of an object that he has secretly chosen, and that is visible to all the players. (They may have to turn their heads in order to see the object, but they should not need to move about.)

For example, if he chose a vase, he would give the letter V or, if he chose a two-word object, the first letter of each word (e.g. PF for picture frame). If the player chooses an object such as a chair, of which there may be more than one in the room, the other players must guess the particular chair he has in mind.

The game ends as soon as someone has spotted the object that was chosen – he may then spy the next object.

Variation I-spy may be played by very young children if colors rather then first letters are given.

For example a player may say "I spy, with my little eye, something red" and the other players then look for the red object that he has in mind.

ANIMAL, VEGETABLE OR MINERAL

Sometimes called Twenty questions, this game is one of the oldest and most familiar word guessing games. Players try to guess an object thought of by one of the others.

Players The game needs two or more players, or two teams. It is often helpful to have a non-playing person to act as referee.

Play One of the players thinks of an object. It may be general (e.g. "a ship"), specific (e.g. "the Lusitania") or a feature (e.g. "the bridge of the Lusitania").

He then tells the others the composition of his chosen object (i.e animal, vegetable, or mineral). The three categories may be defined as follows:

(1) animal: all forms of animal life or anything of animal origin, e.g. a centipede, a tortoiseshell comb;

(2) vegetable: all form of vegetable life or anything of vegetable origin, e.g. flax, a wooden mallet;

(3) mineral: anything inorganic or of inorganic origin, e.g. soda, a mirror.

Objects are often a combination of categories, for example, a can of beer or a leather shoe. (The referee may be consulted if the player is unsure as to the category of an object.)

The player usually indicates the number of words in the object – excluding the definite or indefinite article.

The other players then ask anything up to 20 questions to try to guess the object. They should ask questions of a general nature rather than make random guesses, until they feel confident that they are near to knowing the object.

As each question is put to the player, he must reply either "Yes," or "No," or "I don't know" as appropriate. The referee may intervene if he feels the player has given a wrong or misleading answer; he may also be consulted for guidance on a particular point.

End The first player to guess the object correctly may choose an object for a new round of play. If no one has guessed the object by the time 20 questions have been asked (usually the referee keeps a count) the players are told what it was, and the same person may choose an object for the next round or – if two teams are playing– a person in the other team may choose.

MAN AND OBJECT
In Man and object, a player thinks of a person and something identified with him. The person may be someone known personally to all the players, or a famous personality or fictional character. Examples might be an eskimo and his igloo, or Dante and the inferno.

Playing procedure is the same as for Animal, vegetable or mineral – except that the players might be allowed to ask more than 20 questions.

BOTTICELLI

This game requires a good general knowledge. One person chooses a famous, and tells the other players the initial of his surname. For example, he might say "M" for Groucho Marx.

Taking turns, each player must think of a character whose name begins with that letter, and give a description of him without naming the person he has in mind. If he thought of Mickey Mouse, he would ask "Are you a Walt Disney character?"

If the first player recognises the description, he answers "No, I am not Mickey Mouse," and another player must make a guess.

If the first player does not recognise the description, however, they player who gave it may then ask a direct question that will give him and the other players a lead such as "Are you in the entertainment business?" The first player must give a truthful "Yes" or "No" reply.

The first person to guess the personality wins the round and may choose the next character. If nobody succeeds in guessing the personality after a reasonable length of time, the first player tells them the answer and may choose again for the new round.

WHO AM I?

This is a fairly simple game, in which one player does all the guessing. He may leave the room while the other players think of a well-known personality–real or fictional, dead or alive. The guesser returns to the room and asks "Who am I?" The other players each reply with a clue to the character's identity.

If the character is Napoleon, for example, answers might be;

"You are rather short and stout,"

"You are a great strategist at war,"

"You underestimated the Russian winter."

When each of the players has given a reply, the guesser may make three guesses as to the identity of the person. If he fails to guess correctly, he is told the answer.

Another player is always chosen for the next round.

SCISSORS, PAPER, STONE

This ancient game also known as Hic, haec, hoc, and by many other names, is played all over the world. It is a game for two players.

Three objects (scissors, a piece of paper and a stone) are indicated by different positions of the hand:

(a) two fingers making a V shape represent scissors;

(b) an open hand represents a piece of paper, and

(c) a clenched fist represents a stone.

Each player hides one hand behind his back and adopts one of the three positions. One of the players calls "One, two, three" (or Hic haec, hoc") and as the third word is called the players show their hands.

The winner of a round is decided with reference to the following statements; scissors can cut paper, paper may be wrapped around a stone, and a stone can blunt the scissors.

Thus if one player chooses scissors and the other player paper, the player who chooses scissors wins the round. If both players decide on the same

Scissors, paper, stone: play

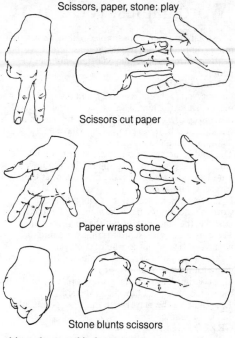

Scissors cut paper

Paper wraps stone

Stone blunts scissors

object, the round is drawn.
Players usually play a pre-determined number of
rounds.

Word games: vocabulary

These games range from simple spelling games to more complex games requiring considerable verbal dexterity. Most can be played by any number of people.

SPELLING BEE

One person is chosen as leader, and the other players sit facing him. The leader may be given a previously prepared list of words or he may make one up himself. It is a good idea to have a dictionary on hand in case of disputes.

The leader then reads out the first word on his list and the first player tries to spell it. He is allowed ten seconds in which to make an attempt at the correct spelling.

If he succeeds, he scores one point and the next word is read out for the next player. If he make a mistake, the leader reads out the correct spelling. The player does not score for that word and the next word is read out for the next player. (Alternatively, the player is eliminated from the game for an incorrect answer.)

Play continues around the group of players until all the words on the list have been spelled.

The winner is the player with the most points at the end of the game.

GREEDY SPELLING BEE

In this version of Spelling bee, whenever a player spells a word correctly he is given another word to spell. Only when he makes a mistake does the next

player take a turn – and he starts with the
incorrectly spelled word.

One point is scored for each correct spelling, and
the player with the highest score at the end of the
game wins.

BACKWARDS SPELLING BEE

In this more difficult version of the Spelling bee,
players must spell their words backwards. Scoring is
the same as in the standard game.

RIGHT OR WRONG SPELLING BEE

The players should form two teams of equal size,
and get in line opposite each other.

The leader calls out a word to each player in turn,
alternating between teams. Each time a player
spells a word, the player standing opposite him
must call out "Right" or "Wrong." If he calls a
correctly spelled word wrong or a misspelled word
right, he is eliminated from the game and must
leave the line. (Players may move around once their
numbers have been depleted, so that there is a
caller for each player in the other team.) If the
caller makes a correct call, he gets the next word to
spell. The last team to retain any players wins the
game.

GHOSTS

Concentration and a good vocabulary are needed to
win this game. Players take it in turns to contribute
a letter to an unstated word, while trying to avoid
completing any word. The first player begins by
thinking of any word (e.g. banana) and calls out the
first letter (B). The next player then thinks of a
word beginning with B (e.g. beetle) and calls out its

second letter (E). Play then continues in this way until one of the players is unable to contribute a letter that does not complete a word. Whenever a player completes a word – and the other players notice – that player loses a "life." This is true even if he completes a word by accident because he was thinking of another word.

If a player is unable to think of a suitable word he may try to bluff his way out of the situation by calling out a letter of an imaginary word. However, if he hesitates for too long or the other players suspect that he has no particular word in mind, they may challenge him. The challenged player must state his word, and if he cannot do so he looses a life. If his explanation is satisfactory, however, the challenger loses a life.

Whenever a player loses his first life he becomes "a third of a ghost". Losing a second life makes him "two-thirds of a ghost" and if he loses a third life he becomes a whole ghost and must drop out of the game.

The game is won by the player who survives longest.

GRAB ON BEHIND

Also called Last and First or Alpha and Omega, this is a good game for a lot of players.

Players decide on a specific category, such as flowers, cities or insects. The first player calls out a word in the chosen category. The next player then follows with another word in the category – but it must begin with the last letter of the previous word. Play continues in this way around the group. For example, if the category were flowers the words might be: mimosa, anemone, edelweiss, sweet pea, and so on.

Players have only five seconds in which to think of a word and may not repeat a word that has already been called.

Anyone failing to think of a word or calling an incorrect word drops out of the round. The last player to stay in wins.

INITIAL LETTER

The players sit in a circle. One of them puts a question – it may be as farfetched as he likes – to the others. Each of them in turn must reply with a two-word answer, beginning with the initials of his or her name. Players have only five seconds in which to think of an answer.

For example, if the question was "What is your favorite food?" Bruce Robertson could reply "Boiled rice," and Robert Chapman might say "Roquefort cheese." When all the players have answered, the second player asks a question. Any player who fails to answer after five seconds or who gives a wrong answer drops out of the game; the winner is the last person to stay in.

INITIAL ANSWERS

This is a good game for a large group of people. The players sit in a circle and one of them starts by thinking of any letter of the alphabet (e.g. S) He must then think of a three-letter word beginning with that letter and give a definition of his word, for example "S plus two letter is a father's child." The second person in the circle has to try and guess the word ("son") and he then thinks of a word of

four letter also beginning with S. He might choose
"soup" and define it as "S plus three letter makes a
tasty start to a meal" for the person sitting next to
him to guess.

This next person after guessing the word correctly,
must think of a five letter word – perhaps "snail"–
defining it as "S plus four letters carries a house on
its back."

The game continues in this way, with each person
having to think of a word beginning with the chosen
letter, and each word having one letter more than the
previous word.

Any player who fails to think of an appropriate
word, or who fails to guess a word must drop out.
The last person left in the game is the winner. A
different letter of the alphabet should be chosen for
the next round.

TRAVELER'S ALPHABET

In this game, the first player says "I am going on a
journey to Amsterdam," or any other town or
country beginning with A. The next person then
asks, "What will you do there?" The verb, adjective
and noun used in the answer must all begin with A;
for example "I shall acquire attractive antiques."
The second player must then give a place using the
letter B, the third player uses the letter C, and so
on, around the players. Any player who cannot
respond is eliminated from the game.

If the players wish to make the game more taxing,
they may have to give an answer that is linked with
the place they have chosen. For example, a player

might say "I am going to Greece to guzzle gorgeous grapes."

If a player gives an inappropriate answer he may be challenged by another player. If that player cannot think of a more fitting sentence, the first player may stay in the game. Should the challenger's sentence be suitably linked, the first player is eliminated.

I LOVE MY LOVE

In I love my love, player have to think of an adjective beginning with each letter of the alphabet to complete a given statement.

The first player starts by saying "I love my love because she is ..." using any adjective beginning with A. The next person repeats the phrase, but his adjective must begin with B, the next person's with C and so on, through the alphabet. Alternatively, each player must make a different statement, as well as using an adjective with a different letter.

Examples of suitable statements are:
"Her name is..."   "She lives in..."
"And I shall give her..."

Players may write down the chosen statements if they wish, but there must be no hesitation over the answers. Any player who hesitates or gives an incorrect answer drops out of the game, and the winner is the last person left in.

I WAS AN APPLE PIE

This is a similar game to I love my love, but players must think of a verb instead of an adjective.

The first player says; "A was an apple pie. A ate it," and other players might add "B baked it," "C chose it," "D dropped it," and so on.

I WENT ON A TRIP

Each player tries to remember and repeat a
growing list of items.

One of the players chooses any article he likes - for
example an umbrella – and says "I went on a trip
and took my umbrella," The next player repeats
the sentence and adds a second item after
"umbrella." In this way the players gradually build
up a list of articles.

Each time his turn comes, a player repeats the list
and adds another item. Whenever a player cannot
repeat the list correctly, the list is closed and the
next player in the group begins a new list.

CITY OF BOSTON

City of Boston is very similar to I went on a trip,
but in this game players must add to a list of items
for sale. Thus the first player might say "I shall sell
you a bunch of violets when you come to the City
of Boston." Each of the other players then repeats
that sentence and adds an item that he will sell.

ONE MINUTE PLEASE

One minute please calls for quick wits and
imagination as players try to speak for one minute
on a given topic. One player is chosen as
timekeeper, and also picks a topic for each player
to talk about.

When it his turn to speak the player is told his
topic. This may be anything from a serious topic
such as "The current political situation" to
something frivolous like "Why women wear hats."
The player may choose to treat the subject in any
manner he pleases and what he says may be utter

nonsense, provided he does not deviate from the topic, hesitate unduly or repeat himself. Other players may challenge the speaker if they feel he has broken a rule. If the timekeeper agrees, then the player must drop out and the next player is given his topic.

The winner is the player who manages to speak for an entire minute. If two or more players achieve this, the others decide which of the speeches was the best, or alternatively further rounds may be played.

ASSOCIATIONS

Associations needs quick thinking, as the slightest hesitation eliminates a player from the game!

One person starts by saying any word (preferably a noun). As quickly as possible, the player next to him says the first word that the first player's word brought to mind, and so on around the group, beginning again with the first player.

If a player hesitates before saying a word, he drops out – if he manages to stay in the game longer than all the other players, he wins.

ASSOCIATION CHAIN

This game can be played as a continuation of the last game. As soon as the chain has formed the last player to have called out a word starts to repeat the chain backwards. If he makes a mistake, he drops out, and the player before him continues to unravel the chain. This goes on until either the first word is reached, or only one player is left.

The more obvious or striking the associations, the easier it is to unravel the chain.

BUZZ

This game should be played as briskly as possible for maximum enjoyment.

The players sit in a circle. One player calls out "One," the next player "Two," the next "Three," and so on.

As soon as the number five, or any multiple of five is reached, the player must say "Buzz." If the number contains a five but is not a multiple of five, only part of it is replaced by buzz. (For example, 52 would be "buzz two.")

If a player forgets to say buzz or hesitates too long he drops out; the last player to stay in the game is the winner.

FIZZ

This is played exactly like Buzz, except that players say "Fizz" for seven or multiples of seven.

BUZZ-FIZZ

Buzz-Fizz combines the two games, so that 57, for example, becomes buzz-fizz.

1 2 3 4 *BUZZ* **6** *FIZZ* **8**

9 *BUZZ* **11 12 13** *FIZZ*

NUMBER ASSOCIATIONS

Number associations needs a person to call out any number between 1 and 12.

As soon as he has said a number, the players call out an appropriate association. For example, if the number called is seven, a player could call "Deadly sins."

The first player to call out a correct association scores one point. Other players may challenge a reply if they feel it is inappropriate. If the leader agrees with the challenge, that player loses one point from his score.

An association may not be repeated. At the end of the game, the winner is the person with the highest number of points.

TABOO

In Taboo - sometimes called Never say it - players try to avoid saying a particular letter of the alphabet. One player is the questioner and chooses which letter is to be "taboo."

He then asks each of the players in turn any question he likes. The respondent must answer with a sensible phrase or sentence that does not contain the forbidden letter - if he does use the taboo letter, he is out.

The last player to stay in the game wins and becomes the next questioner.

BUZZ 161 FIZZ 18 19 BUZZ

Dice

Dice games were played in ancient times and remain universally popular. Here we look at ways of passing a happy hour with little or no gambling involved.

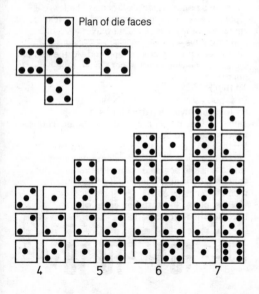

Plan of die faces

4   5   6   7

Dice A standard modern die is a regular cube, with the six sides numbered with dots from 1 through 6. Any two opposite sides add up to 7.

Odds With one true die, each face has an equal chance of landing face up. With two dice thrown together, some scores are more likely than others because there are more ways in which they can be made.

Possible throws
with two dice

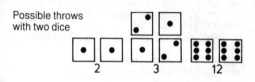

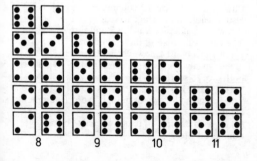

FIFTY

This game, for two or more players, is one of the simplest dice games. It requires two dice, and the winner is the first player to score 50 points.

Each player in turn rolls the two dice, but scores only when identical numbers are thrown (two 1s, two 2s and so on). All these doubles, except two 6s and two 3s, score five points. A double 6 scores 25 points, and a double 3 wipes out the player's total score and he has to start again.

ROUND THE CLOCK

This is a game for three or four players, using two dice.

Objective Players try to throw 1 through 12 in correct sequence. The winner is the first to complete the sequence.

Play Players throw both dice once on each turn. From 1 through 6, a player can score with either one of the two dice or with both of them – e.g. a throw of 3 and 1 can be counted as 3, 1 or 4. It is also possible at this stage to score twice on one throw – e.g. if a player needs 2 and throws a 2 and a 3 he can count both of these numbers.

From 7 through 12, however, a player will obviously always need the combined spot values of both dice to score.

SHUT THE BOX

This is a game for two or more players. Equipment:
(1) two dice.
(2) a board or piece of paper with nine boxes numbered 1 to 9;

Shut the box:
sample play

6 + 4 = 10 thrown
8 + 2 = 10 covered

(3) nine counters used to cover the boxes in play
(In some parts of the world, specially made trays
with sliding covers for the numbers are available.)
Objective Players aim to cover as many of the
numbers as possible, in accordance with the throws
of the dice. The winner is the player with the lowest
penalty score from uncovered boxes.
Play The player taking first turn throws the two
dice and then decides which boxes he will cover. He
may cover any two boxes that have the same total
as his throw – e.g. a throw of 10 would allow him to
cover 6 and 4, 7 and 3, 8 and 2 or 9 and 1.
The same player then throws the two dice again
and tries to cover another two boxes. He is not
allowed to use combinations involving numbers
that he has already covered.
After covering boxes 9, 8 and 7 a player may throw
only one die on a turn, but he must still cover two
boxes at a time.
A player's turn continues until he is unable to make

use of a combination from his last throw. All the uncovered numbers are then added up and become his penalty score.

Play then passes to the next player.

DROP DEAD

This is an exciting game for any number of players. Equipment:

(1) five dice;

(2) paper on which to record players' scores.

Objective Players aim to make the highest total score.

Play At his turn each player begins by rolling the five dice. Each time he makes a throw that does not contain a 2 or a 5, he scores the total spot value of that throw and is entitled to another throw with all five dice.

Whenever a player makes a throw containing a 2 or a 5, he scores nothing for that throw and any die or dice that showed a 2 or a 5 must be excluded from any further throws that he makes. A player's turn continues until his last remaining die shows a 2 or a 5 – at which point he "drops dead" and play passes to the next player.

CHICAGO

Chicago, also called Rotation is a game for any number of players. Two dice are used. The game is bases on the 11 possible combinations of the two dice – 2, 3, 4, 5, 6, 7, 8, 9, 10, 11 and 12 – as so consists of 11 rounds.

The objective is to score each of these combinations in turn. The player with the highest score is the winner.

Play Each player in turn rolls the dice once in each round. During the first round, he will try to make a total of 2, during the second, a total of 3, and so on up to 12.

Each time he is successful, that number of points is added to his score. For example, if he is shooting for 5 and throws a total of 5 he gains five points. If he fails to make the desired number, he scores nothing on that throw.

PIG

This simple game, for any number of players, requires only one die. The winner is the first player to reach a previously agreed high score (usually 100).

Order of play is determined by a preliminary round. Each player throws the die once and the player with the lowest score becomes first shooter. The next lowest scoring player shoots second and so on. The order of play is important because the first and last shooters have natural advantages (see below).

Pig: sample play
Player 1

Stops, scores 24

Player 2

Out

Play begins with the first shooter. Like the other players, he may roll the dice as many times as he wishes. He totals his score throw by throw until he elects to end his turn. He passes the die to the next player, memorizing his score so far.

But if he throws a 1, he loses the entire score he has made on that turn, and the die passes to the next player. Play passes from player to player until someone reaches the agreed total.

Given a little luck, the first shooter is the player most likely to win. But his advantage can be counteracted by allowing other players to continue until they have had the same number of turns. The player with the highest score is then the winner.

The last shooter still has the advantage of knowing the scores made by all his opponents. Provided he does not roll a 1, he can continue throwing until he has beaten all other scores.

The fairest way of playing the game is to organize it as a series, with each player in turn becoming first shooter.

GOING TO BOSTON

Also known as Newmarket or Yankee grab, this game is ideal for three or four players.

Equipment: three dice.

Play Each player in turn rolls the three dice together. After the first roll he leaves the dice showing the highest number on the table, then rolls the other two again. Of these, the die with the highest number is also left on the table and the remaining die is rolled again. This completes the player's throw; the total of his three dice is his score. When all players have thrown, the player with the highest score wins the round. Ties are settled by further rolling.

A game usually consists of an agreed number of rounds; the player who wins the most rounds is the winner.

Alternatively, each player can contribute counters to a pool that is won at the end of each game.

MULTIPLICATION

This game is played like Going to Boston, but with one important difference. When each player has completed his turn, his score is the sum of the spot values of the first two dice rolled, multiplied by that of the third. For example, if his first throw is 5, his second throw 4, and his final throw 6, his score will be 54: $(5 + 4) \times 6$.

BEETLE

This is a lively game for two or more players – more than six tend to slow down the game.

Equipment:

(**1**) 1 die, either an ordinary one or a special "beetle die" marked B (body), H (head), L (legs), E (eyes), F (feelers) and T (tail);

(**2**) a simple drawing of a beetle as a guide, showing its various parts and (when an ordinary die is used) there corresponding numbers;

(**3**) a pencil and a piece of paper for each player.

Objective Each player, by throwing the die, tries to complete his drawing of the beetle. The first to do so scores 13 points and is the winner. The 13 points represent one for each part of the beetle (body, head, tail, two feelers, two eyes and six legs).

Beetle: scoring

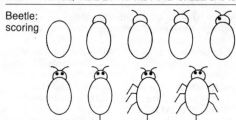

Play Each player throws the die once only in each round. Each player must begin by throwing a B (or a 1); this permits him to draw the body.

When this has been drawn, he can throw for other parts of the beetle that can be joined to the body. An H or a 2 must be thrown to link the head to the body before the feelers (F or 5) and eyes (E or 4) can be added. Each eye or feeler requires its own throw.

A throw of L or 3 permits the player to add three legs to one side of the body. A further throw of L or 3 is necessary for the other three legs.

Sometimes it is agreed that a player may continue to throw in his turn for as long as he throws parts of the body he can use.

Continuing play When a series of games is played, each player counts one point for every part of the beetle he has been able to draw and cumulative scores are carried from round to round.

The winner is the player with the highest score at the end of the series, or the first to reach a previously agreed total score

HEARTS

Hearts, or Hearts due, is a game for two or more players.

Equipment Six dice are used. Special dice marked with the letters H, E, A, R, T, S instead of numbers are sometimes used, but the game is now more commonly played with ordinary dice.

The objective is simply to score more than your opponents over an agreed series of round, or a single round, or to be the first to reach an agreed total.

Play begins after a preliminary round has decided the first shooter (the player with the highest score). Each player in turn rolls the six dice once and calculates his score according to the following ratings:

1(H) = 5 points;
1,2 (HE) = 10 points;
1,2,3 (HEA)= 15 points;
1,2,3,4 (HEAR) = 20 points;
1,2,3,4,5 (HEART)= 25 points;
1,2,3,4,5,6 (HEARTS)= 35 points.

If a double (two dice of the same spot value) or a triple appears in the throw, only one of the letters or numbers counts. But if three 1s (or Hs) appear, the players whole score is wiped out and he has to start again.

CENTENNIAL

Also known as Martinetti or Ohio, this is a game for two to eight players.

Equipment:

(1) three dice;

Centennial: scoring

Everest: scoring

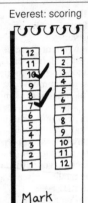

Mark

(2) a long board or piece of paper marked with a row of boxes numbered 1 to 12;

(3) a distinctive counter or other object for each player.

Objective Each player tries to be the first to move his counter, in accordance with throws of the dice, from 1 to 12 and back.

Play begins after a preliminary round had determined who will take the first turn. Each player on a turn throws all three dice at one. Turns pass clockwise around the table.

In order to place his counter in the first box, a player must throw a 1. He can try then for a 2, a 3, and so on, box by box up to 12 and back again. He can make any number with one or more dice. For example, a 3 can be scored with one 3, a 1 and a 2, or with three 1s. It is possible to move through more than one box on a single throw. For example, a throw of 1, 2, 3 would not only take him through the first three boxes, but on through the fourth (1 + 3 = 4), to the fifth (2 + 3 = 5) and finally the sixth (1 + 2 + 3 = 6).

Other players' throws must be watched constantly. If a player throws a number he needs but overlooks and does not use, that number may be claimed by any other player. He must do this as soon as the dice are passed, however, and must be able to use it at once.

EVEREST

This game is like Centennial but has a different layout and scoring system.

Equipment Each player has a sheet of paper showing two columns, each divided into 12 boxes. In one column, the boxes are numbered from 1 to 12 in ascending order. In the other they are numbered from 1 to 12 in descending order.

Objective Each player tries to be the first to score all 24 numbers. the numbers do not have to be scored consecutively as in Centennial, but as desired and in either column.

Scoring Each die in a throw can be counted only once.

DICE BASEBALL

As a dice game for two player, baseball can be played in several different ways. A popular version

Dice baseball:
sample play

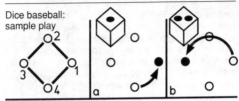

using one die is described here.

Equipment:

(1) one die;

(2) at least three counters for each player to represent his men;

(3) a sheet of paper with a simple diagram of a baseball diamond drawn on it;

(4) another piece of paper for recording scores.

The objective is to score the highest total number of runs in the nine innings per player that constitute the game. If the two players have equal scores after the usual nine innings, and extra-inning game is played. (Note than in baseball, each player's turn at bat is called a "half-inning.")

Order of play The players throw the die to decide who shall "bat" first (i.e. shoot the die first). Each player in turn then throws a half-inning. A half-inning is ended when a player has thrown three "outs" (see below).

Making runs At the start of the game, or whenever all bases are empty, a throw of 1, 2, or 3 permits the player to put a man (counter) on whichever of those three bases he has thrown – 1 in the example illustration (**a**).

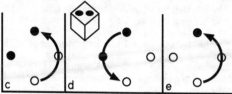

If the player throws 1, 2 or 3 again, this permits him
to move the man around the diamond by the number
of bases thrown, and to place another man on the
base that bears the number thrown. For example, if
he has a man on 1, and throws a 2, the man advances
to base 3 (**b**) and a new man is entered on base 2 (**c**).
Each time a man reaches the home (fourth) base or
"home plate," a run is scored. A single throw may
give a score of more than one run if it takes more
than one man to home base.

For example, if a player with men on bases 2 and 3
throws a 2, both men advance to home base and two
runs are scored (**d**).

At the same time a new man is entered on base 2
(**e**). A throw of 4 counts as a home run and advances
all men on the bases to home base. The score is thus
the home run plus one run for each man brought
home.

Outs Throws of 5 or 6 are "outs."

A throw of 5 is as though there had been a hit and a
force out, so that men on the bases may also be out,
as follows;

if the shooter has only one man on the bases, he is
out;

if he has men on all bases, the man on base 1 is out;
if he has men on bases 1 and 2, the man on base 2 is
out;
if he has men on bases 1 and 3, the man on base 3 is
out;
if he has men on bases 2 and 3, both are safe.
Men on the bases who are not out remain where
they are.
A throw of 6 is also an out, but it is as if the batter
were out without striking the ball; men on bases are
safe, and remain where they are.
Note that three outs end a half-inning. The other
player then throws his half-inning to complete the
inning.

DICE BASKETBALL

As a dice game, basketball is usually played by two
players, but more can take part, each player
representing a team. As in the real game, the
winner is the team (i.e. player) making the highest
score in the game or series of games.

Equipment Basketball may be played with only
two dice or with as many as 10. Many players use
eight dice as there are then enough to ensure a
rapid game and realistic scores.

Play A game consists of four quarters. In each
quarter, each player in turn rolls the eight dice
once, their total being his score for that quarter. If
the game is played with only two dice, each player
rolls the dice four times to determine his score for
that quarter.
The player with the highest score for the four
quarters wins the game. If the game, or agreed

series of game, ends in a tie, this is resolved by playing extra quarters until the outright winner is established.

CHEERIO

This game can be played by any number of players up to maximum of 12. The greater the number of players, the slower the pace of the game.

Equipment:

(1) five dice;

(2) a dice cup;

(3) a piece of paper showing the various combinations and with a scoring column for each player.

Objective Each player tries to score the maximum possible for each of the 11 scoring combinations (see p.141). The player with the highest total score wins the game.

Games are often played as a series, the player who wins the most games in the series being the overall winner.

Alternatively, the scores in each game can be carried forward to the next game until a player has reached a previously agreed cumulative total. If two or more players exceed the total, the player with the highest score wins.

Ties are settled by an extra game.

Play Each player in turn rolls all five dice. Having rolled the dice once, he may pick up all or any of them and roll once more in an attempt to improve his score.

He does not have to try for combinations in any particular order, and he does not have to declare his combination until he has finished rolling. This gives him a considerable freedom of choice. For example, if he has rolled 6, 6, 2, 3, 3 he might call sixes (score 12). But if he wanted to keep sixes for a later turn, when he might roll more than two of them, he could call a different combination even if this would give him a lower score or even no score for the throw.

A player is not permitted to call the same combination more than once in a game.

Combinations

Ones Scores one point for each die showing one spot (maximum score 5 points).

Twos Scores two points for each two-spot die (maximum 10).

Threes Scores three points for each three-spot die (maximum 15).

Fours Scores four points for each four-spot die (maximum 20).

Fives Scores five points for each five-spot die (Maximum 25).

Sixes Scores six points for each six-spot die (maximum 30).

Little straight A show of 1, 2, 3, 4, 5 scores 20 points.

Big straight A show of 2, 3, 4, 5, 6 scores 25 points

Full house Three of a kind plus two of a kind scores according to the numbers shown on the dice (6, 6, 6, 5, 5 scores the maximum 28 points).

Big hand The total spot value of the dice (6, 6, 6, 6, 6 scores the maximum 30 points).

Cheerio Five of a kind in any value, 1 through 6, Always scores 50 points.

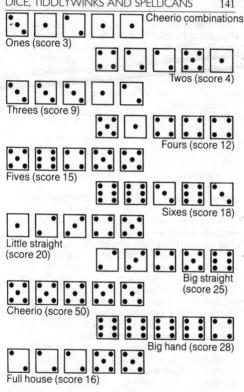

Cheerio combinations

Ones (score 3)

Twos (score 4)

Threes (score 9)

Fours (score 12)

Fives (score 15)

Sixes (score 18)

Little straight (score 20)

Big straight (score 25)

Cheerio (score 50)

Big hand (score 28)

Full house (score 16)

GENERAL
This game has many similarities with Cheerio
(p.139). It is a major gambling game in Puerto
Rico, but can also be played without stakes.
Equipment:
(1) 5 dice;
(2) a score card showing combinations and players'
names .
Players Any number may play, either singly or in
partnership.
Objective Each player or partnership aims to win
by scoring a "big general" (see five of a kind) or by
scoring most points for the 10 General
combinations. As in Cheerio, each combination
may be scored only once in a game.
Order of play is determined by a preliminary round
in which each player rolls the dice once. The player
with the lowest spot score shoots first, the player
with the next lowest score second, and so on.
Play A game normally consists of 10 turns
("frames") per player but ends immediately if any
player rolls a big general. Each player may roll the
dice once, twice or three times during each frame.
If, on his first throw, he fails to make a combination
that he wishes to score, he may pick up all or any of
the dice for second roll. But the value of any
combination he now rolls is diminished, and a big
general now becomes a small general.
After his second roll, he may again, if he wishes,
pick up all or any of the dice for a third roll. After
the third roll, he must state which combination he
is scoring.

General

Play then passes to the next player.

If the game runs its full course of ten frames, the player with the highest score wins.

Aces wild "Aces" (1s) may be counted as 2 or as 6 if one or both of these are needed to complete a straight – but not as any other number or for any other purpose.

Combinations

Numbers 1 through 6 Score their spot values.

Straight Either 1 ,2, 3, 4, 5 or 2, 3, 4, 5, 6 scores 25 points if made on the first throw, but only 20 points if made on the second or third throw. Only one straight is scored.

Full house Scores 35 points on first throw, but only 30 points on the second or third throw.

Four of a kind Scores 45 points on first throw, but only 40 points on the second or third throw.

Five of a kind If made on the first throw, it ranks as the "big general" and immediately wins the game. Made on the second or third throw it is a "small general" and scores 60 points.

Payment When General is played as a gambling game, the winner receives from each of the other players the difference between his own and that player's point score. The monetary value per point is settled before the game.

DOUBLE CAMEROON

This game is similar to General but has important differences.

It is played with ten dice.

After a player has rolled them for the third time in each turn, he divides them into two groups of five,

and then allots the score of each group to one of
the ten combinations in the game. So in the course
of a game, each player has five turns.

Combinations

Number 1 through 6 Score their spot values.

Full house Scores its spot value.

Little Cameroon (1, 2, 3, 4, 5) scores 21 points.

Big Cameroon (2, 3, 4, 5, 6) scores 30 points.

Five of a kind scores 50 points.

(Unlike in General, a score does not decrease if the
combination is made on a second or third throw.)

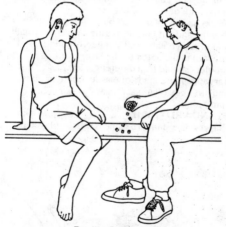

Double Cameroon

Tiddlywinks

In the standard game of Tiddlywinks, each player attempts to put small discs or "winks" into a cup by shooting them with a larger disc called a "shooter." Variations include games based on sports such as Tennis and Golf.

Playing area Games are played on the floor or on a table. Any shape of table may be used but a square or round one is best if there are more than two players. The table should be covered with a thick cloth or piece of felt.

Winks and shooters must be slightly pliable and are usually made of bone or plastic. Winks are usually about ⅝in. (1.5cm.) and shooters around 1in. (2.5cm.) in diameter. Each players winks and shooters should be a different color.

Target cups are made of plastic, wood ,or glass and are 1½in. (4cm.) across and 1 – 2in. (2.5cm. – 5cm.) high.

STANDARD GAME

Players The standard game is usually played by

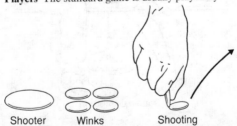

Shooter   Winks   Shooting

two, three or four players.

Equipment Each player usually has a shooter and four winks. A target cup is also needed.

Objective The game is won by the first player to get all his tiddlywinks in the cup.

Start of play The cup is placed in the center of the playing area, and each player places his winks in a line in front of him.

Turns Order of play is often decided by a preliminary shot – first shot of the game going to the player who gets his wink nearest the cup. Play is then usually clockwise around the players.

Each player shoots one wink in a turn plus one extra shot each time he gets a wink into the cup.

Shooting A player shoots a wink by stroking and pressing the edge of the shooter against the edge of the wink and so making the wink jump into the air. A wink is shot from where it lies after the player's previous turn.

Out of play Any wink that is partly covered by another is out of play. A player whose wink is covered by an opponent's wink must either wait until the opponent moves his wink or must attempt to remove the opponent's wink by hitting it with one of his own winks.

Any wink that stops against the side of the cup is out of play until it is knocked level onto the table by another wink.

A wink that is shot off the table does not go out of play. It must be replaced on the table at the point where it went off.

Scoring Tiddlywinks may be scored in two ways;
(a) players count the number of games they win;
(b) players score one point for each wink in the cup
when each game ends.

PARTNERSHIP TIDDLYWINKS
Tiddlywinks can be played by partners in the same
way as the standard singles game except that:
players pair up with the player sitting opposite;
partners play alternately and may play either their
own or their partner's winks.

FORFEIT TIDDLYWINKS
An interesting variation of the standard game is
played by drawing six concentric circles around the
cup. Play is the same as for the standard game
except that any wink that lands in one of the circles
is forfeited and immediately removed from the
table.

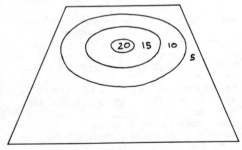

Target Tiddlywinks

TARGET TIDDLYWINKS GAME

These variations involve shooting winks at numbered targets.

Typical layouts are;

(a) a target with concentric circles each worth a set number of points;

(b) a raised target with numbered scoring areas.

Target Tiddlywinks games are played in the same way as the standard game except that:

players score a set number of points for landing their winks on different parts of the target (a wink touching two scoring areas always scores the lower number);

a wink may not be shot again once it has landed on any part of the target, but may be knocked by another wink.

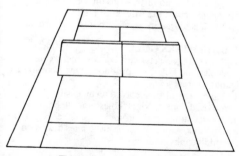

Tiddlywinks tennis (see p.150)

TIDDLYWINKS TENNIS

The lines of a tennis court should be marked on the
floor or the tiddlywinks cloth. (Dimensions for the
court should be varied to suit the skill of the players
and the height of the net.) An improvised net can
be made with folded paper or card, or with a row of
books.

Players shoot a wink back and forth over the net –
gaining points whenever their opponents fail to get
the wink over the net or shoots it so that it goes
outside the limits of the court.

The game can be played by two players (singles) or
four players (doubles). In the doubles version,
partners take turns to shoot the winks from
their side of the net.

Rules for service can be modified to suit the skill of
the players – e.g. extra shots allowed to get the wink
over the net or no restrictions on where in the
opponent's court the wink must land.

A match is scored in games and sets as in ordinary
tennis.

TIDDLYWINKS GOLF

Tiddlywinks golf sets, with tiddlywinks, greens,
obstacles and holes, are produced by various toy
manufacturers.

The game can also be played on an easily
improvised course. Nine "holes" should be
positioned at intervals around the course. Holes can
be egg cups, napkin rings or just circles drawn on
the tiddlywinks cloth.

Tiddlywinks golf

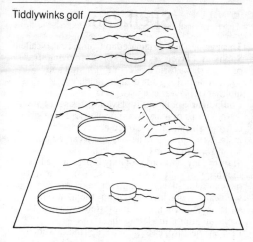

The course is then made more interesting by the addition of obstacles – such as rumpled or corrugated paper under the cloth to make rough ground, upturned books to make raised ground, and box or jar lids for water obstacles. The game can be scored by "stroke" or by "hole" as in real golf. In the first, each player counts the number of shots he takes to complete the course. In the second, players score one for each hole won and a half for each hole tied.

Spellicans

This game, which originated in China, is also called Spillikins. Players try their skill at removing straws or small sticks form a pile, one at a time and without disturbing any of their neighbors. Any number of players can take part.

Equipment Spellicans is played with a set of about 30 thin strips of ivory, wood or plastic. These strips, called spellicans, have carved heads representing animals, people, etc. There is also a carved hook for moving the strips.

Start of play The order of play is determined by the throw of a die or some other means. The last person in the playing order then takes all the spellicans in one hand and drops them onto the table or floor. He must not interfere with any spellican after it has left his hand.

Play At his turn, each player takes the carved hook and attempts to remove a spellican from the pile without disturbing any of the others. Once a player has started moving a particular spellican he is not permitted to transfer his attack to a different spellican.

If he successfully removes a spellican from the pile, he keeps it and tries to remove another spellican from the pile. A player's turn continues until he disturbs a spellican other than the one he is attacking.

Play continues in this way until all the spellicans have been taken.

Scoring Each spellican has a points value, and a game is won by the player with the highest score. Spellicans that are generally fairly easy to move have a low value, and more elaborate and difficult to move spellicans have a correspondingly higher value.

PICK-UP-STICKS

The game is similar to Spellicans. Alternative names are Jackstraws/Jerkstraws, Juggling sticks, and Pick-a-stick.

Equipment Pick-up-sticks is played with about 50 wood or plastic sticks or straws. These are about 6in. (15cm.) long, rounded, and with pointed ends, and colored according to their point value.

Play The rules are the same as for Spellicans except that players remove the sticks with their fingers or, in some versions of the game, may use a stick of a specified color after they have drawn one from the pile.

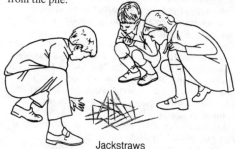

Jackstraws

Dominoes

Games with dominoes are played in many countries all over the world. They are now particularly popular in Latin America. It is thought that dominoes may have been brought from China to Europe in the fourteenth century. Certainly domino games were played in Italy in the eighteenth century. In most Western games, players add matching dominoes to a pattern or "layout" formed in the center of the table.

Players Some domino games are for two players only. Others are for two or more players, playing alone or as partners:

Partnerships may be decided:

(a) by mutual agreement;

(b) by draw – in which case each player draws one domino and the two players with the heaviest dominoes form one pair.

Partners sit opposite each other at the table.

Playing area Dominoes can be played on a table or any other flat surface.

The dominoes are rectangular tiles made of wood, ivory, bone, stone or plastic. They are sometimes called "bones," "stones," or "pieces." A typical size is 1in. (2.5cm.) by 1⅞in. (4cm.) by ⅜in. (1cm.). Each domino's face is divided by a central line and each half is either blank or marked with indented spots (sometimes called "pips"). Dominoes with the same number of spots on either side of the central line are called "doubles" or "doublets".

A domino is said to be "heavier" than another if it

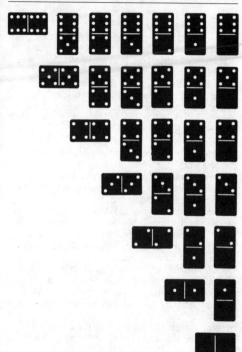

has more spots, or "lighter" if it has fewer spots. So a double 6 is heavier than 6:5.

The standard Western domino set has 28 tiles (with double 6 the heaviest domino) Larger sets have 55 dominoes (double 9 the heaviest) or 91 dominoes (double 12 the heaviest).

Suits Dominoes belong to different suits according to the number of spots on each of their halves. There is a suit for each number, a blank suit and a double suit.

"Mixed number" dominoes belong to two number suits or to a number suit and the blank suit.

Doubles belong to one number suit and to the doubles suit.

General features of play Western domino games are characterized by the principle of matching and joining dominoes end to end.

In some games, players add dominoes to either end of a line of dominoes. More common are games in which players may build on four ends of a pattern or "layout." In one game, Sebastopol (p.163), the layout has up to eight ends.

Doubles in most games are placed across the line of dominoes and in some rules (e.g. Tiddle-a-wink, p.161) a player who, for example, plays a double 6 may immediately play another common domino with a 6 at one end.

In some games, players use only the dominoes picked up at the start of play, and must miss a turn

(called "renouncing," "passing," or "knocking")
whenever they are unable to add a matching
domino to the pattern. In other games, players
must draw a domino from a reserve of downward-
facing dominoes (called the "boneyard") whenever
they are unable to play a matching domino.

General rules No domino may be withdrawn after
it has been added to the layout.

If the wrong domino is accidentally placed face up
by a player during his turn, it must be played if it
matches an end of the layout.

A player is liable to lose the game if:

(a) he fails to play within two minutes;

(b) he renounces when he is able to play;

(c) he plays a domino that does not match (except
that the domino is accepted if the error is not
noticed before the next domino is played);

(d) he makes a false claim that he has played all his
dominoes.

Drawing a hand All the dominoes are placed face
downward in the center of the table and are then
moved around by all the players. Each player now
selects the number of dominoes required for the
game to be played – usually seven or five.

Dominoes rack

Except in the few games in which players do not look at their own dominoes (e.g. Blind Hughie, p.161) players may keep their dominoes standing on edge on the table, on a rack or concealed in their hand.

Turns There are several ways of deciding which player is to have the first turn.

(a) The player who draws the heaviest domino in a preliminary draw is the first to play.

(b) One player draws a domino and his opponent guesses whether its spots add up to an odd or even number.

(c) Each player draws his dominoes for the game and the first turn goes to the player with the heaviest double or, if there are no doubles, to the player with the heaviest domino.

In most countries, turns then pass clockwise around the table, in Latin America, the direction of play is counter-clockwise.

End of play Games end:

(a) when one player has played all his dominoes – after which he calls, "domino!" or makes some other recognized signal;

(b) when no player can add a matching domino in games with no drawing from the boneyard;

(c) in drawing games when no player can add a matching domino and only two dominoes remain in the boneyard.

Result Most games are played to a set number of points. In some games, the player who first plays all his dominoes claims one point for each spot on his opponents' unplayed dominoes.

If all play is blocked, the player with fewer spots on his unplayed dominoes claims the difference between the number of spots on his own and his opponents' unemployed dominoes. The hand is replayed if the opponents dominoes have an equal number of spots.

In other games (e.g. Bergen, p.168), players score points adding a domino that makes the two ends of the layout match.

BLOCK DOMINOES

The basis Block dominoes game is usually played by two, three or four players using a standard set of 28 dominoes. (More players can play with larger sets.) Two players usually play with seven dominoes each. and three or four players with five dominoes each. The first player begins by laying any of his dominoes face up in the center. Turns then pass around the table – with players adding matching dominoes to either end of the line or missing a turn if none of their dominoes match.

Spots are counted and points scored after one player has played all his dominoes or the game is blocked so that no one can play (see Result, opposite) The winner of one hand plays first in the next hand. A game is usually played to 100 or 200 points.

PARTNERSHIP BLOCK DOMINOES

The partnership form of Block dominoes is played
by four players with a standard set of 28 dominoes.
Play is the same as for basic Block dominoes
except that:

(a) players sitting opposite one another form a
pair;

(b) each player draws seven dominoes at the start
of the game;

(c) the player with the double six starts the first
hand by laying it on the table;

(d) subsequent hands are started by the winner of
the previous hand and this player may play any of
his dominoes to start;

(e) pairs score jointly – as soon as one player has
played all his dominoes, he and his partner score
the sum of the spots on each of their opponents'
unplayed dominoes;

(f) in blocked games, the pair with the lowest total
of spots on their unplayed dominoes scores the
difference between their own and their opponents'
total of spots on their unplayed dominoes.

LATIN AMERICAN MATCH DOMINOES

This Latin American form of dominoes is played in
the same way as Partnership block dominoes
except that:

(a) the player with the double 6 always starts;

(b) each hand won counts as one game;

(c) a match ends when one pair has won 10 hands;

(d) a match is scored only if the other pair failed to
win five hands – otherwise the match is tied.

DOMINO POOL

The rules of standard Block dominoes apply to
Domino pool except that, before each hand, players
place equal bets in a pool or pot. The winner of the
hand takes all; or if players tie, they share the pot
between them.

TIDDLE-A-WINK

This is a form of Block dominoes particularly suited
to larger groups of people. It is often played with
sets of 55 or 91 dominoes.

At the start of each hand the dominoes are shared
out equally between the players; any remaining
dominoes are left face downwards on the table. Play
proceeds as for the basic Block game except that:

(a) the player with the highest double always starts;
(b) any player who plays a double may add another
domino if he is able;
(c) a player who has played all his dominoes calls
"tiddle-a-wink".

(Another version of the game is played by six to
nine players with three dominoes each from a set of
28 dominoes. In this version, dominoes are added to
only one side of the starting double and bets are
made as in Domino pool.)

BLIND HUGHIE

Blind Hughie is a Block dominoes game of chance.
If four or five players are playing with 28 dominoes,
each draws five dominoes without looking at them;
two or three players each draw seven dominoes.
Each player lays his dominoes in a line face
downwards in front of him.

The first player starts by taking the domino at the

left of his line and laying it face up in the center of the table.

Turns then pass around the table. At his turn each player takes the domino at the left of his line and;

(a) if it matches an end of the layout, he plays it;

(b) if it doesn't match, he lays it face downwards at the right of his line.

Play continues until one player finishes his dominoes or until the game is obviously blocked.

DRAW DOMINOES

Draw dominoes is characterized by the drawing of dominoes from the boneyard after the start of play. Players usually start with seven or five dominoes each. Play is as for basic Block dominoes except that:

(a) a player who is unable or unwilling to add a domino to the layout must draw dominoes from the boneyard until he draws one that he is able or willing to play, or until only two dominoes remain in the boneyard;

(b) when only two dominoes remain in the boneyard, a player who cannot play a domino must end or miss a turn;

(c) a player who draws or looks at an extra domino, or who turns a domino up so that other players see it must keep that domino.

DOUBLES

This game, also called Maltese Cross, is played in the same way as basic Draw dominoes except that:

(a) the player with the heaviest double leads;

(b) play is on four ends from the starting double;

(c) a player may add a mixed number domino only

Doubles

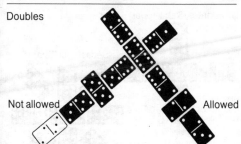

Not allowed   Allowed

if the double of the number he is matching has
already been played (e.g. in the hand illustrated, a
player could add 2:3 to the double 2 but could not
play the 3:2 on the 5:3).

FORTRESS, SEBASTOPOL, CYPRUS

These are names for two closely related games.

(a) The first game usually called Fortress but
sometimes called Sebastopol, is a Block dominoes
game for four people with 28 dominoes. Each
player draws seven dominoes and the player with
the double 6 starts (see p.159).

Play is on four ends from the double 6 and a
domino must be added to each of these ends before
play proceeds as for standard Block dominoes.

(b) The second game, more usually called
Sebastopol but sometimes called Cyprus, is a Draw
dominoes game played with a set of 55 dominoes.
Four or five players start with nine dominoes each;
more players start with seven or five.

Double 9 always starts and if no player has this

Fortress/Sebastopol

Sebastopol/Cyprus

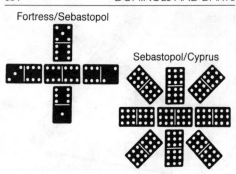

domino, players should draw one domino in turn until someone draws it. Play is on eight ends from the double 9, and all ends must be opened before a second domino may be added to any end.

Players draw one domino from the boneyard if they are unable to add a domino to the layout.

ALL FIVES

This game, also called Fives Up, is a form of Draw dominoes that is particularly popular in the United States. It is an interesting game characterized by its scoring system based on multiples of five.

Using a 28-domino set, two three or four players start with five dominoes each. The first player may lead with any domino – and scores if its ends add up to a five (a) or 10 The next player scores if the ends of the layout still add up to five or a multiple of five

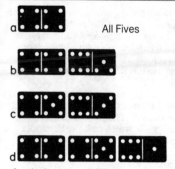

a   All Fives

b

c

d

after he has played (b). If he is unable to score, he may play another domino (e.g. the 1:3, which would make the ends of the layout add up to seven), or may draw one domino from the boneyard.

The first double of the game (c) opens up a third end (in this case there would be no score since 6 + 6 + 4 = 16).

The next domino (d) opens up the fourth and final end of the layout and in this case it scores since 6 + 6 + 4 + 4 = 20). Play continues on four ends of the layout until one player finishes all his dominoes or until the game is blocked.

Scoring In one version of the game, a player scores one point for each spot whenever the layout's ends total five or a multiple of five. The winner of a hand also scores points for the spots on his opponents' remaining dominoes. Game is usually 150 or 200 points.

More usual, however, is the scoring system in which
players score one point when the ends total five,
two points for 10, three points for 15 and so on.
The winner of the hand scores a fifth of the face
value of his opponents' remaining dominoes. In
this version, the game is won by the first player to
score exactly 61 points.

If a player fails to claim his points after playing a
domino, the first opponent to call "fives" claims
those points for himself. The game is sometimes
played by partners – in which case the dominoes
left in the losing partner's hand are ignored for
scoring purposes.

ALL THREES

All threes, or Three up, is played in the same way
as All fives but scoring is based on multiples of
three.

FIVES AND THREES

This is played in the same way as All fives, but
scoring is based on multiples of both five and three.
A player scores one point for each spot whenever
the ends of the layout total five or a multiple of
five, or three or a multiple of three. If a number is
a multiple of both five and three, the player scores
two points for each spot. The winner also scores for
each spot on an opponent's remaining dominoes.

MATADOR

In this unusual draw game, dominoes are played
when they make a specified total with a domino on

an end of the layout. There are also wild dominoes called "matadors" that can be played at any turn. These are versions of the game for different sizes of domino sets.

When a 28 domino set is used, added dominoes must make a total of seven, and the matadors are the 6:1, 5:2, 4:3 (i.e. those with ends totalling seven), and the 0:0.

Matador 55 set

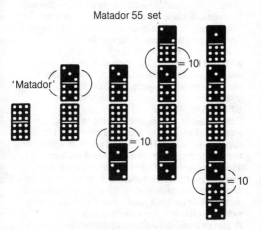

For a 55 set the required total is 10 and the matadors are the 9:1, 8:2, 7:3, 6:4, 5:5 and 0:0. (In the game illustrated, play opened with the double 9. This was followed by the 7:3, a matador, and then by

three dominoes making totals of 10.) For a 91 set
the total is 13 and the matadors are the 12:1, 11:2,
10:3, 9:4, 8:5, 7:6 and 0:0.

Players usually start with seven or five dominoes
each, depending on the number of players and the
size of set. The player with heaviest double starts.
In this game doubles are not placed crossways and
the layout has only two ends.

If a player is unable or unwilling to add a domino,
he must draw one domino from the boneyard.
When only two dominoes remain in the boneyard,
he must play a domino if he is able.

A had is won by the player who finishes his
dominoes or who holds dominoes with the fewest
spots if the game is blocked. Points are scored for
the spots on an opponent's remaining dominoes,
and the game is an agreed number of points.

BERGEN

Bergen is a Draw dominoes game in which players
score points when there are matching dominoes. at
the ends of the layout. Using a set of 28 dominoes,
two or three players start with six dominoes each
and four players with five dominoes each. The
player with the highest double starts. Subsequent
play is on two ends only, and a player who is unable
or unwilling to add a domino to the layout must
draw one domino from the boneyard.

A player scores two points whenever two ends of
the layout match (a "double heading") – as, for
example the 6:2 and the 3:2 in the illustration (i.e.
before the addition of the double 2). A player
scores three points for a "triple heading" – i.e. when

Bergen

there is a double at one end and a matching domino at the other, as after the addition of the double 2 in the example illustrated.

A player scores two points for a winning hand. If no player finishes his dominoes, and the game is blocked, the hand is won by the player holding no doubles, the player with fewest doubles, or the player with fewest spots on his dominoes. Game is usually 10 or 15 points.

FORTY TWO

Forty-two or Domino rounce, is an adaptation of a card game for play with dominoes. The object is to score points by winning tricks.

The game is usually played by four players with a set of 28 dominoes. Play is usually with partners. Each player draws seven dominoes at the start of a hand.

Bidding is the first stage of play, and tricks are valued as follows:

(a) one point for each trick taken;

(b) five additional points for a trick containing the 5:0, 4:1 or 3:2 (i.e. the dominoes with a total of five spots each);

(c) 10 additional point for a trick containing 5:5 or 6:4 (i.e. ten spots each).

The total tricks value is 42 points (and hence the name of the game).

The player holding the 1:0 domino makes the first

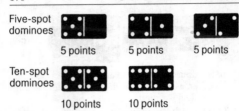

Five-spot dominoes

5 points   5 points   5 points

Ten-spot dominoes

10 points   10 points

bid, and the other players bid in turn. Players may make only one bid and no bid may be for less than 30 points or be lower than a preceding bid. A player may pass if he does not wish to bid.

Taking tricks The player or pair with the highest bid then attempts to take tricks worth the value of their bid (or more).

There are eight suits – blanks, the numbers 1 to 6 and doubles. Except when a trump is led, the highest number on a domino determines the suit. The highest bidder plays the first domino and this establishes the trump suit for the hand. If he leads a "mixed number" domino, he calls out which number is the trump suit. The other players then play one domino in turn.

Except when a trump or a double is played, a trick goes to the player who played the heaviest domino of the correct suit. A double is the strongest domino of its suit, and can be taken only by a trump. As in card games, a higher number in the trump suit takes a lower one.

The player who takes a trick always leads for the next trick.

Taking tricks

In the examples illustrated:

(a) double 3 takes the trick – scores five extra points because the 3:2 is taken;

(b) if 2s are trumps, the 2:1 takes the trick – and scores 10 extra points because the 6:4 is taken.

Scoring If the bidder and his partner make tricks worth as many or more points than the bid, they score the full value of their tricks plus the number of points bid.

If the bidder and his partner fail in their objective, their opponents score the number of points bid plus the value of the tricks that they have made.

DOMINO BINGO

This is another game in which dominoes are used like playing cards and players score points for making tricks.

It is a game for two players with a set of 28 dominoes. Players make preliminary draw to determine who will lead for the first trick.

At the start of play, each player draws seven dominoes from the boneyard. The leader then establishes trumps for the hand by turning over a domino in the boneyard. This domino is left exposed and its highest number becomes the trump suit for the hand.

The leader for the first trick then plays one domino and his opponent follows him. There is no need for a player to follow suit, except when the game is "closed" or the boneyard is empty.

Taking tricks The double blank, called "bingo," takes any other domino.

If two trumps are played, the higher trump takes the trick.

If one trump is played, the trump takes the trick. If no trumps are played, the heaviest domino wins the trick.

If no trumps are played and both dominoes have the same total spots, the leader's domino takes the trick.

As long as any dominoes remain in the boneyard, each player draws a domino after each trick. The winner of a trick always draws first and then leads on the next trick.

When only two dominoes remain in the boneyard, the winner of the preceding trick may take the trump domino or the domino that is face down, and the losing player takes the remaining domino.

Value of tricks There is no score just for taking a trick. The value of a trick depends on the dominoes it contains. Only the following dominoes have any points value (with 2s as trumps in the example illustrated):

(a) the double of trumps is worth 28 points;

(b) except when blanks are trumps, "bingo" is worth 14 points;

Value of tricks (2s trumps)

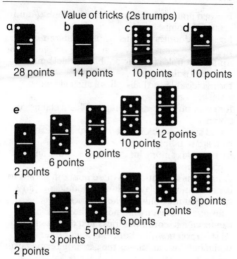

a
28 points

b
14 points

c
10 points

d
10 points

e
2 points
6 points
8 points
10 points
12 points

f
2 points
3 points
5 points
6 points
7 points
8 points

(c) the 6:4 is worth 10 points;

(d) the 3:0 is worth 10 points;

(e) other doubles are worth their total number of spots;

(f) trumps other than the double are worth their total number of spots.

Value of doubles A player can also claim points for having more than one double in his hand at any time when it is his turn to lead. To claim these points he should play one double and expose the others.

For two doubles in his hand he call "double" and
claims 20 points;

for three doubles he calls "triple" and claims 40
points;

for four doubles he call "double doublet" and
claims 50 points;

for five doubles he calls "king" and claims 60
points;

for six doubles he calls "emperor" and claims 70
points;

for all seven doubles he calls "invincible" and
claims 210 points;

if "bingo" is among his doubles he claims an extra
10 points.

A player is not entitles to these points if he fails to
claim them when laying down a double; nor do
they count if he fails to take the trick.

Closing If a player with the lead believes that he
can bring his score from tricks and doubles to at
least 70 points without drawing any further
dominoes, he can "close" the game by turning over
the trump domino.

After the game is closed neither player may draw
any further dominoes and rules for following suit
come into force.

Following suit After the game is closed or the
boneyard is empty, a player is obliged when
possible to follow suit.

If a trump is lead he must play another trump. If a
domino that is not a trump is led, he must try and
follow its higher number or, failing that, its lowest
number. If he can not follow neither of these, he

may play a trump. Only if he has none of these is her permitted to discard.

Scoring A game is won by the first player to score seven sets of game points.

Sets are scored as follows:

(a) one set for every 70 points from tricks or doubles:

(b) one set for being the first player to reach 70 points if the other player has at least 30 points;

(c) two sets for reaching 70 points after the other player has taken a trick but has not scored 30 points;

(d) three sets for reaching 70 points before the other player takes a trick;

(e) one set for taking the double of trumps with "bingo."

DOMINO CRIBBAGE

This game is an adaptation of playing card cribbage. The basic domino game is for two players, using a standard set of 28 dominoes. As in the card game, the score is usually kept on a cribbage board.

Objective The game is won by the first player to score 61 points. Scoring takes place during play and also at the end of a hand.

Play Each player draws six dominoes at the start of play, discarding two of them, face downwards, to form the crib, an extra hand scored by the dealer after the other hands have been scored.

The leader then turns over a domino in the boneyard. This domino is the "starter." It is not used during play but is scored with all hands after play.

Turns alternate. The leader's opponent begins by placing any domino from his hand face upwards on the table in front of himself and calling out its total number of spots.

The leader then turns over one of his dominoes and calls out the sum total of spots on both dominoes played so far.

Play proceeds in this way, with each player calling the sum total of spots played, until the "go" rule comes into play. If, at his turn, a player is unable to play a domino that will bring the count to 31 or below, he must call "go." The other player must then play as many tiles as he can until he reaches 31 or is unable to play.

Once a count of 31 has been reached, or if no one can play, a new count from 0 begins. (Pairs, etc., cannot be carried over into the next count.)

After both players have played all their dominoes, the leader's opponent scores the points in his hand. The leader then scores the points in his hand and then the points in the crib. The lead then passes to the other player and another hand is started.

Scoring during play For turning up a double for starter, one point.

For reaching a count of exactly 15, two points. For a "pair" (playing a domino with the same total spot count as the last played domino), two points;

For a "triplet" (a third domino with the same total spot count) six points;

For a fourth domino with the same spot count, 12 points.

For a run of three or more dominoes, not

Scoring during play

 Double for 'starter', 1 point

 15, 2 points

 Pair, 2 points

 Run, 3 points

necessarily in order (e.g. dominoes totalling 7, 8, 9), one point for each tile of the run.

For reaching exactly 31, two points.

For being nearer to 31, one point.

For the last tile of the hand, one point.

For reaching 15 with the last tile, three points.

Scoring after play For a combination totaling 15, two points.

For a double run of three (a three-tile run with a pair to one of them) eight points.

For a double run of four (a run of four with one pair) 10 points.

For a triple run (a triple with two other dominoes in sequence), 15 points.

For a quadruple run (two pairs and a domino in sequence with both), 16 points.

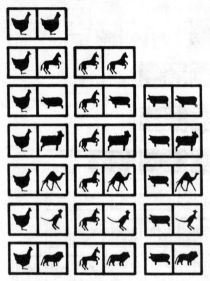

PICTURE DOMINOES
Dominoes with pictures are very popular with young
children and can be easily bought or made. A typical
set contains 28 brightly colored dominoes with
combinations of seven different pictures. They are
usually made of wood or cardboard.
All the dominoes are shared out among the players,
who should keep the pictures hidden from the other

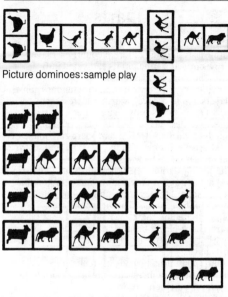

Picture dominoes: sample play

players. One player starts by placing one domino
face upwards on the table. Players then take turns
at adding a matching domino.
If a player doesn't have a matching domino, he
misses his turn.
The winner is the player to add all his dominoes to
the row on the table.

Darts

A traditional English "pub" game. Darts now has
enthusiasts in many different countries. Players
throw darts at a circular target divided into
different scoring areas. Games are played by
individuals, pairs, or teams. In the standard game,
players aim to reduce a starting score exactly to
zero. Other games provide a greater variety of
objectives designed to test the players' skill.

Standard dartboard Most dartboards are made of
cork, bristle, or elm, with the divisions and sector
numbers marked by wires.

The standard tournament board is 18in. (45.5cm.)
in diameter and twenty sectors, an outer "doubles"
ring an inner "triples" ring, and an inner and outer
"bull" in the center. Adjacent sectors are
differentiated by color.

Darts Each player has a set of three darts. Designs
vary but most darts are about 6in. (15cm.) long. All
darts have:
a sharp point usually made of steel;
a barrel, made of metal (usually brass), or plastic
weighted with metal, or wood;
a tail, "flighted" with feathers, plastic, or paper.

The scoreboard is a slate or blackboard, usually
positioned to one side of the dartboard. Each side's
score is recorded in chalk.

Playing area The dartboard is hung on a wall, with
the center 5ft. 8in. (1.74m.) from the ground. Toe
lines may be marked on a mat or on the floor, at

8ft. (2.4m.), 8ft. 6in. (2.6m.), and 9ft. (2.7m.) from the dartboard.

STANDARD TOURNAMENT DARTS

Players Games are played by individuals, pairs or teams of any fixed number of players.

Starting Each player, or one member of each pair

or team, must get a dart in the doubles ring to begin
scoring. The starting double scored, as are darts
thrown after but not before it in the same turn.
Turns In singles games, opponents take turns to
throw three darts each. In pairs and team games,
one player from each side throws three darts in turn,
with members of each side playing in the order

Playing area

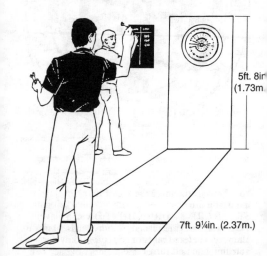

5ft. 8in
(1.73m

7ft. 9¼in. (2.37m.)

established at the start of the game.

The first turn goes to the player, pair, or team that wins the toss of a coin or gets a dart nearest the bull in a preliminary throw.

Scored throws A throw is illegal if the player is not behind the toe-line when throwing.

Only those darts sticking in the board at the end of a player's turn are scored. Thus darts are not scored if they rebound, stick in another dart, fall from the boards, or are knocked out before the player ends his turn.

Re-throws are not permitted. (Also note starting and finishing procedures.)

inner bull

outer bull

b   a

Scoring Scored throws are deducted from a starting total – usually 301, 501, or 1001.

Darts in the inner bull score 50, and in the outer bull 25. Darts in a sector score according to the sector number – unless they are within the outer (doubles) ring (a) when they score double the sector number, or the inner (trebles) ring (b), when they score three times the sector number.

Finishing The game ends with a double bringing the score exactly to zero. If the score in a player's turn take him past zero, or to one, he goes back to the score, before that turn and forfeits any darts remaining in that turn.

AROUND THE CLOCK

This is a singles game for any number of players.
Each player throws three darts in turn.

After a starting double, each player must throw one
dart into each of the sectors, in order, from 1 to 20.
Darts in the doubles or trebles rings of the correct
sector are usually allowed. The winner is the first
player to finish.

As a variation, players may be awarded an extra
turn for scoring with the last dart of a turn.

SHANGHAI

Shanghai is another "round the clock" game for any
number of players with three darts each.

In his first turn, each player throws all his darts at
sector number 1. Singles, doubles and trebles all
score their value. In his second turn, each player
throws all his darts at sector number 2 (even if he
made no score in his first turn).

Play proceeds in this manner right "around the
clock" and the winner is usually the player with the
highest total score.

In a popular variation of this game, a player may
win by going "Shanghai" (i.e. by scoring in one turn
a single, double, and treble of the required number).

CLOSING

This is a game for two players, each with three darts.
Each player aims to make as high a score as possible
while seeking to prevent his opponent from making
a high score.

As soon as one of the players has scored three times
from any one sector, that sector is "closed" and no
further score may be made from it by either player.

Closing sample scoreboard

	A	B
20	✱✱✱	✕✕
19		✱✱✱
18	✕ ✕	✕
17		
16	✱✱✱	✕✕
15		
14	✕	
13		✕✕
12	✕	
11		
10		
	170	175

Doubles and trebles score their value, and count as two and three scores respectively. The winner is the player with the highest score when the last sector is closed.

SCRAM

Scram is a game for two players throwing three darts in each turn.

The player with the first turn is the "stopper," and any sector he hits with a dart is closed to his opponent.

The second player is known as the "scorer," and he aims to score as many points as possible before all the sectors are closed.

When all the sectors are closed, the two players change roles. The winner is the player who scores most when playing scorer.

KILLER

Killer is probably best with four to eight players, but can be played by either more or less.

In his first turn, each player throws one dart with the hand that he normally does not use for throwing darts. This throw decides a player's own sector for the rest of the game. Unless a very large number of people are playing, it is usual for a player to throw again if a sector has already been given to another player.

In every other turn, each player throws three darts with his usual hand. The game has several versions, but in all cases the winner is the player left in the game when all other players have lost all their "lives."

First version In one version of the game, all players begin with no lives and a player's objective is to acquire three lives by throwing three darts into his own sector (two lives for a double and three for a treble).

Once a player has three lives, he becomes a "killer" and starts throwing darts at other players' sectors. (In the example illustrated, players B and C become killers after their second turns and player A after the first throw of his third turn.)

If a killer throws a dart into sector of a player with three or two lives, that player loses one life (or two for a double or three for a treble).

If a killer throws a dart into the sector of a player with one or no lives, that player is out (player B after C's third turn in the example illustrated).

A killer who loses a life loses his right to kill until he makes up his lost life by throwing another dart into his own sector.

Second version All players start with an agreed number of lives – usually three or five. To start killing, a player has to throw a double of his own number. Kills are made by throwing doubles and

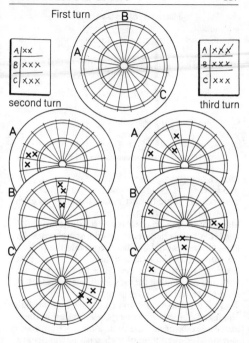

First turn

second turn

third turn

trebles of other players' numbers – one kill for a double and two kills for a treble. Lost lives cannot be won back again.

Half it sample scoreboard

	A	B
20	/	20
19	19	39
18	17	75
DOUBLE	18	105
17	4	122
16	4	61
15	19	30
TREBLE	9	40
14	4	45
13	10	71
12	15	95
DOUBLE	7	48
TREBLE	3	49
11	25	60
10	35	80
BULL	17	40

HALVE IT

Halve it is a game for any number of players, each throwing three darts in a turn.

Before play begins, players select a series of objectives and chalk them up on a scoreboard. A typical series would be 20,19,18 any double, 17, 16, 15, any treble, 14,13,12, double, treble, 11, 10, bull. In his first turn, each player aims for 20 and scores for each dart in that sector (doubles and trebles count their value).

Players then take turns to make their way through the list of objectives, scoring for each dart in the correct sector or halving their total score (rounding down) whenever none of their darts scores. There are no minus scores, and a player whose score is reduced to zero stays at zero until he throws a dart that scores.

FIVES

Fives can be played by two players or sides using a standard dartboard. The winner is the first player to reach an agreed number of points, usually 50.

Each player throws three darts in a turn. He scores only if the sum of his three darts can be divided by five – in which case he scores the result of this division.

A player who throws a dart out of the scoring area when he has a total divisible by five, scores no points for that turn.

DARTS FOOTBALL

This is a game for two players, each throwing three darts in turn.

A dart in the inner bull "gains control of the ball." This player can then start scoring "goals"– one for each double.

He continues scoring until his opponent "takes the ball away" by scoring an inner bull, The first player to score ten goals wins the game.

DARTS CRICKET

Darts cricket is a game for two teams of equal size. The team that wins the toss of a coin decides whether to "bat" or to "bowl." Turns alternate between teams, and each player throws one dart in a turn.

When "batting," a team aims to score as many "runs" as possible; when "bowling," to "take wickets" by scoring inner bulls.

The team change roles after five wickets are taken. The team with the highest batting score wins the game.

DARTS BASEBALL

This is a game for two players, each representing a baseball team,

There are nine innings, and each player has a turn at "bat" in each inning. A player's turn consists of three throws.

In the first inning players throw darts at sector 1, in the second inning at sector 2, through to sector 9 in the ninth inning. Extra innings are played if there is a tie.

A single "run" is scored by getting a dart into the correct sector for the inning (with two runs for a double and three for a treble). Getting a bull at any stage of the game is a "grand slam home run" and scores four runs.

DARTS SHOVE HA'PENNY

This game for two players, or pairs is based on the rules of the board game. Each player throws three darts in turn, and the objective is to score three times in each of the sectors numbered 1 to 9.

The scores may be made in any order, and doubles count as two scores and trebles as three.

If a player scores more than three times in any one sector, the extra scores are given to the opposition. The score that wins the game, however, must always be actually thrown by the winner. The game is won by the first side to finish.

Darts shove ha'penny

A	B	
■	●	
	✓	1
✓✓		2
	✓	3
✓✓		4
✓✓		5
	✓	6
		7
		8
✓✓✓	✓	9

Checkers

Known as Checkers in the USA and Draughts in the UK, this is a popular board game for two players. It was played in Southern Europe in medieval times and appears to have been derived from much older games played in the Middle East. Each player attempts to "take" (capture and remove) his opponent's pieces or to confine them so that they cannot be moved.

Board The game is played on a board made of wood, plastic, or cardboard and 14½ to 16in. (36 – 40cm.) square. It is divided into 64 squares, eight along each side. The squares are alternately a light and a dark color (usually black and white, or sometimes black and red or red and white) Play is confined to squares of only one color – usually the darker color.

Pieces Each player has a set of 12 pieces – wooden or plastic discs 1¼ – 1½ in. (3.25cm.–3.5cm.) in diameter and about ⅜in. (1cm.) thick. One set is usually white, and the other red or black.

Objective A player aims to "take" all his opponent's pieces or to position his own pieces so that his opponent is unable to make any moves.

Start of play The players sit facing each other, and the board is positioned so that the players have a playing square at the left of their first row. Lots are drawn to decide who will have the darker pieces for alternate games.

Start of play

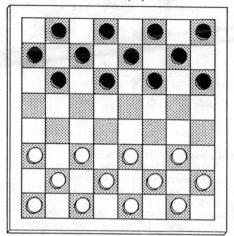

For the start of play each player positions his pieces on the playing squares in the three rows of the board nearest to him. The player with the darker pieces always makes the first move in the game.
Moving A player may make only one move at a turn. As play is confined to squares of only one color, all moves are diagonal. Individual pieces or "men" may only be moved forward (a); double pieces or "kings" may be moved either forwards or backwards (b) (see over page).

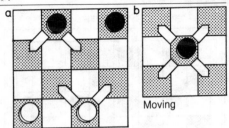

Moving

A piece may only be moved into a square that is vacant.

Touch and move Except when he has given notice of his intention to arrange pieces properly in their squares, a player whose turn it is must, when possible, make his move with the first piece that he touches.

If he first touches an unplayable piece, he is cautioned for a first offence and forfeits the game for a second offence.

Time limit for moves If a player fails to make a move within five minutes, an appointed timekeeper shall call "time." The player must then move within one minute, or forfeit the game through improper delay. (At master level in some tournaments, players must make a prescribed number of moves within set time limits.)

A non-taking move Except when "taking" an opponent's piece, a player may only move a piece into a touching playing square.

A taking move One of the game's objectives is to "take" (capture and remove) the opposing pieces.

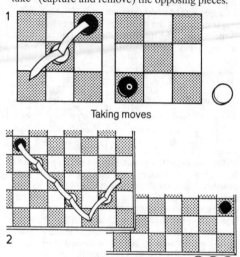

Taking moves

A piece may be taken if it is in a playing square touching the taker's square when there is a vacant square directly beyond it (1) Several pieces can be taken in one move provided that each one has a vacant square beyond it (2)

Whenever possible, a player must make a taking move rather than a non–taking move (even if this means that his own piece will in turn be taken). If a player has a choice of taking moves he may take a smaller instead of a larger number of pieces (3a), but if he begins the move enabling him to take the larger number he must continue until he has taken all the pieces possible (3b).

3a

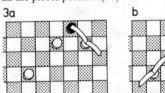

b

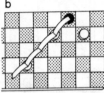

Failure to take If a player fails to take a piece when he is able (1a) modern tournament play rules state that his opponent should point this out and so force him to take back the wrongly moved piece and make the taking move instead (1b).

This ruling has replaced the old "huff and blow" rule, by which a player who failed to make a possible taking move forfeited the piece moved in error.

Failure to take

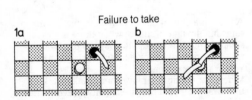

1a   **b**

Crowning When a man reaches the farthest row of the board (known as the "king row," or "crownhead,") it becomes a "king" and is "crowned" by having another piece of its own color placed on it (2). A player's turn always ends when a man is crowned.

2a   b

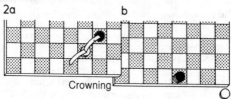

Crowning

A tied game occurs when neither player can remove all his opponent's pieces or prevent him making a move (3a,3b).

If one player appears to be in a stronger position, he may be required to force win within 40 of his own moves or else place himself at a decided advantage over his opponent. If he fails, the game is counted as tied.

3a   b

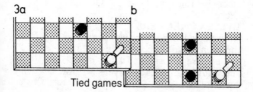

Tied games

TOURNAMENT CHECKERS

To reduce the number of tied and repeated games
at expert level, a system of restricted openings is
applied at major championships and tournaments.
The first three moves of each game are determined
by card bearing the various openings and
subsequent moves. The cards are shuffled and cut,
and the top card is turned face up. Opposing
players then play two games with the prescribed
opening, each player making the first move in one
of the games.

LOSING/GIVEAWAY CHECKERS

This is played under the same rules as standard
American or British checkers. The tactics, however,
are very different, as the objective is to be the first
player to lose all his pieces.

DIAGONAL CHECKERS

This is an interesting variant of the standard game.
It can be played with 12 pieces per player, in which
case starting position (a) is used, or with nine
pieces each if starting position (b) is used. Men are
crowned when they have crossed the board to
reach the opponent's corner square (marked K in
the diagram).

Otherwise, rules are the same as for standard
checkers.

ITALIAN CHECKERS

This is played in the same way as standard
American or British checkers except that:

(a) the board is positioned with a non-playing
square at the left of each player's first row;

Diagonal checkers; alternative start

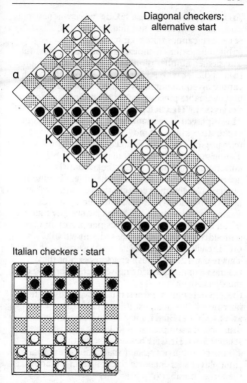

Italian checkers : start

(b) a player must make a taking move whenever possible – or forfeit the game;

(c) a man cannot take a king;

(d) if a player has a choice of captures he must take the greater number of pieces;

(e) if a player with a king to move has a choice of capturing equal numbers of pieces, he must take the most valuable pieces (i.e. kings rather than men).

SPANISH CHECKERS

This is played in the same way as Italian checkers, except that kings are moved differently. A player may use a king to take a piece anywhere on a diagonal, provided that there are no pieces between and there is an empty square beyond it. The jump need not end in the square immediately behind the taken piece, but may continue any distance along the diagonal if there are no intervening pieces (a). A king must make all his jumps before any taken pieces are removed, and these pieces may not be jumped a second time in the same move (b).

GERMAN CHECKERS

This is played as Spanish checkers except that;

(a) men can make taking moves either forward or backwards;

(b) a man is only crowned if its move ends on the far row – if it is in a position to make further jumps away from that line it must always take them and thus not be crowned.

RUSSIAN CHECKERS

This is played like German checkers except that:

(a) a player with a choice of captures need not take the larger number of pieces;

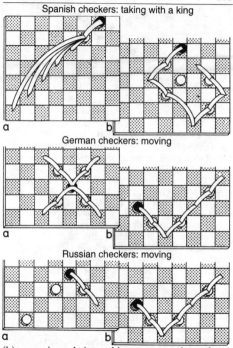

Spanish checkers: taking with a king

a   b

German checkers: moving

a   b

Russian checkers: moving

a   b

(b) a man is made into a king as soon as it reaches the far row and then jumps as a king for the rest of the move.

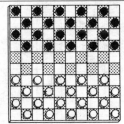

CONTINENTAL CHECKERS

Also called Polish checkers, this is played on a board with 100 square, 10 along each side. Each player has 20 pieces – positioned on the first four rows for the start of play. The game is played under same rules as German checkers.

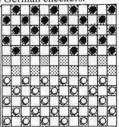

CANADIAN CHECKERS

This is another variant of German checkers. It is played on a board with 144 squares, 12 by 12. Each player has 30 pieces – positioned on the first five rows for the start of play.

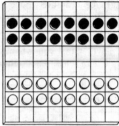

TURKISH CHECKERS

This may be played on a standard checkers board, but the traditional Turkish board has squares all the same color. Each player has 16 pieces – positioned on each player's second and third rows for the start of play.

Men move as in American or British checkers, but directly forwards or sideways and not diagonally (a). Kings move any number of squares directly forwards, sideways, or backwards. Multiple captures by kings are made as shown (b) – as for Spanish checkers except that moves are not diagonal and pieces are removed as soon as they are jumped (instead of staying on the board to prevent further jumps).

A player must make a capture whenever possible, and must always take the greater number of pieces when he has a choice of captures.

Turkish checkers may be won in the usual ways, and also by a player with a king when his opponent has only a single man remaining on the board.

Chequers
Go-Moku:
won game

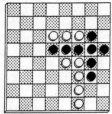

CHECKERS GO-MOKU

This is an adaptation of a Japanese game which is a version of a Chinese board game. Play is on all the squares of a standard checker board, and the two players have 12 pieces each.

The board is empty at the start of a game, and the players take it in turns to place one piece on any square. After all the pieces have been placed, a player uses his turn to move one piece into any vacant, adjoining square.

If, at any stage of the game, a player succeeds in placing five pieces in a row (horizontally, vertically or diagonally), he is entitled to remove any one of his opponent's pieces from the board.

The game is won when a player has removed all his opponent's pieces.

Checkers Fox and Geese: alternative starts

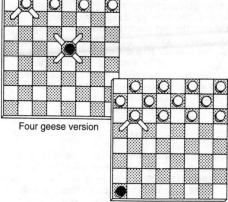

Four geese version

Twelve geese version

CHECKERS FOX AND GEESE

Two versions of an old game known as Fox and
Geese are often played on a checkers board and
are particularly popular with children.

In both checkers versions, one player has one dark
piece (the "fox") and his opponent has several
white pieces (the "geese").

Play is only on the black squares of the board. A
player moves only one piece at a turn. The fox wins
the game if it can break through the line of geese.
The geese win if they can trap the fox so that it
cannot move.

FOUR GEESE VERSION

At the start of play, the player with the geese
positions them on the four playing squares of his
first row; the player with the fox positions it
wherever he chooses.

The geese move diagonally forward on square at a
time like the men in American or British checkers.
The fox moves diagonally forwards or backwards; it
is not permitted to jump over the geese, so there is
no taking in this version.

TWELVE GEESE VERSION

This version is sometimes played with a "wolf" and
"goats." At the start of play, the geese are positioned
on the first three rows, as for American or British
checkers; the fox is positioned on one of the corner
playing squares on the opposite side of the board.

The geese move like the men and the fox like a king
in American or British checkers. (Jumping and
taking geese is permitted in this version.)

Chess

Originating in the East over a thousand years ago, Chess has developed into one of the most popular of all games. Despite being highly complex and sophisticated, it can also be enjoyed at a simpler level by inexperienced players. It is a game of strategy for two people, with each piece – from the king to the pawn – representing units in an army.

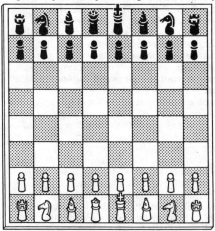

The board is a large square divided into eight rows of eight squares each. The squares are alternately

dark and light colored (usually black and white).
The board is placed between facing players so that
each has white square at the right-hand corner. The
row of squares running vertically between facing
players are called "files," those running at right
angles to the files are called "ranks." Rows of
squares of the same color that touch only at their
corners are called "diagonals."

Pieces At the start of a game, 32 pieces are
positioned on the board. Sixteen of these pieces are
dark in color, 16 light. They are called black and
white respectively and make up the two sides.
A player's side is made up of six different kinds of
pieces. These are – in descending order of
importance: king, queen, rook (castle), bishop,
knight, pawn. Each player has one king and one
queen, two castles, bishops and knights and eight
pawns.

Objective The objective of each player is to capture
his opponent's king. Unlike the other pieces, the king
cannot be removed from the board; it is held to be
captured when it has been "checkmated" (see
section on check and checkmate, p.216).
The player forcing checkmate wins the game – even
if the pieces he has left on the board are
outnumbered by the opponent's pieces.
A player seeing the imminent checkmate of his king
or recognizing a losing situation will often resign.
The player forcing the resignation wins the game.

Moves Each kind of piece can move a certain
distance in one or more directions. Moves are limited
by conditions on the board at the time of play.

Names of rows

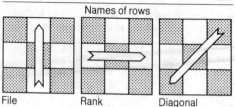

File   Rank   Diagonal

A piece may move to any square within its range provided that:

(a) the square is unoccupied by a piece of its own color;

(b) if the square is occupied by an opponent's piece, that piece is first "captured" and removed from the board;

(c) it does not, with the exception of the knight's move, cross a square that is occupied by a piece of either color.

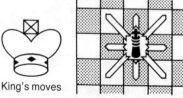

King's moves

The king is the most important piece on the board, and its capture by checkmate ends the game. It is represented diagrammatically by a crown.

The king can move one square in any direction,

provided that this square is not one where it can be taken. Opposing kings can never stand on touching squares.

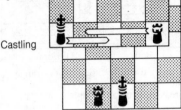

Castling

Castling The only time that a king may move more than one square is in the "castling" move involving the rook. A player can make a castling move only once in a game. The move is made to produce a defensive position around the king and to allow a rook to come into play. It comprises:
(1) moving the king two squares to left or right from its original position and towards one of the rooks: then
(2) transferring that rook to the square over which the king has just passed.
Castling is permitted only if:
(a) neither the king nor the rook involved has moved from its original position;
(b) no piece of either color is between the king and the rook involved in the castling move;
(c) the square that the king must cross is not under attack by an opponent's piece.

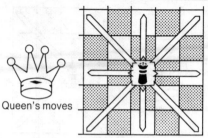

Queen's moves

The queen, represented diagrammatically by a coronet, is the most powerful attacking piece. It can move to any square on the rank, file or either of the two diagonals on which it is placed.

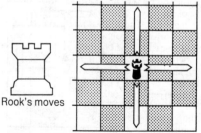

Rook's moves

The rook, sometimes called the castle, is represented diagrammatically by a tower. It can move to any square on the rank or file on which it is placed.
In addition, either one of the rooks in each side may be involved with the king in the castling move.

Bishop's moves

The bishop, represented diagrammatically by a mitre, can move to any square on the diagonal on which it is placed. Thus each player has one bishop that can move on a black diagonal and one on a white diagonal.

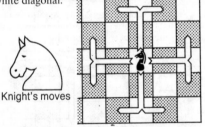

Knight's moves

The knight is represented diagrammatically by a horse's head. In a single move, it travels two squares in any direction along a rank or file, then one square at right angles to that rank or file. Thus whenever a knight moves from a black square it must land on a white square – and vice versa.

In moving, a knight may cross a square occupied by any other piece; it is the only piece allowed to do so.
The pawn, represented diagrammatically by a small ball on a collared stem, has the most restricted movements of any piece; it can only move forwards.

Pawn's ordinary move   Alternative opening move

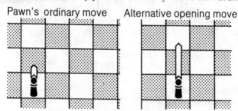

In its opening move, a pawn may be moved forward either one or two squares on the file that it occupies. Thereafter, a pawn can only move forward one square at a time, except when capturing.

Capturing move

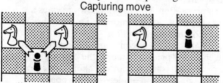

Unlike other pieces, a pawn does not capture in the same way that it moves. Instead of capturing in a forward direction, it does so diagonally – taking a piece that occupies either of the two squares diagonally next to it.

Capture "en passant"

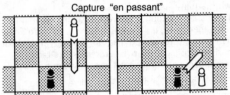

In addition, a pawn may capture an opposing pawn
"*en passant*" (in passing). If the opposing pawn
moves forward two squares in its opening move, the
square it crosses is open to attack as though the
pawn had only advanced one square. Thus the
capturing pawn may make its usual taking move (i.e.
one square, diagonally forward) onto the square just
crossed by the opposing pawn– the opposing pawn
is then considered "captured" and is removed from
the board. (The "en passant" capture must be made
immediately the opposing pawn has moved forward
two squares.)

Pawn promotion Whenever a pawn reaches the end
of the file on which it is moving (i.e. it reaches the
far side of the board) it must – in the same move –
be exchanged for a queen, rook, bishop or knight.
The choice of piece is made by the player promoting
the pawn, and is made without taking into account
the number and kind of pieces on the board.
Theoretically, therefore, a player could have up to
nine queens on the board.
The effect of the promoted piece on play is
immediate.

Starting procedure Players draw for sides, and

position their pieces on the board. The player
drawing white makes the first move, and thereafter
the players move alternately.

Play The position of the pieces at the start of play is
such that each player can move only a knight or a
pawn. After the first move by each player, more
pieces can come into play.

In moving their pieces, players are governed not
only by the movements laid down for each piece but
also by the rules that affect how pieces can be
handled. If a player touches a piece that can
legitimately be moved, then he must move that
piece – unless he has previously warned his
opponent that he is adjusting the piece on its square.
The usual warning used is "*J'adoube*" (I adjust).
Similarly, if a player touches an enemy piece that
can be taken, the touched piece must be captured
unless the player has given prior warning.

Capturing move

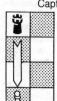 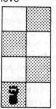

A move is completed when:
(a) a player's hand has left a piece after it has been
moved to a vacant square;

(b) a player, having captured a piece and placed his attacking piece on the captured square, removes his hand from the piece;

(c) in castling, a player's hand has left the rook (once the king has been moved, the castling move must always be completed);

(d) in pawn promotion, a player's hand has left the piece that replaces the pawn.

Phases of play Chess players commonly divide a game into three phases: opening game, middle game, and end game. These phases are not clear cut divisions – they simply reflect the strategies and tactics employed.

(1) In the opening game, both players position their pieces into what each considers to be an advantageous situation. Castling moves are usually made during this phase.

(2) In the middle game, players attempt to capture enemy pieces, thereby reducing the opponent's attacking ability. However, as the main objective is to checkmate the opponent's king, moves or captures should not be made unless they weaken the opponent's defence of his king. The player should also beware of making moves that jeopardize his own position.

(3) In the end game, players attempt to checkmate the opponent's king. If, during this phase, a player has few attacking pieces, he will attempt – where possible – to promote a pawn to a more powerful piece.

Check and checkmate Whenever a king is attacked by an opposing piece, the king is said to be "in

Check   a   b   c

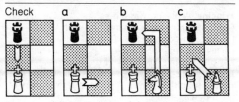

check." The check must be met on the following move by either:

(a) moving the king one square in any direction onto a square that is not attacked;

(b) capturing the piece that is checking the king; or

(c) interposing a piece between the king and the attacking piece (if the king is checked by an opponent's knight, it is not possible to intercept the check in this way). A piece that intercepts a check can – in the same move – give check to the opposing king.

If the check cannot be met then the king is deemed "in checkmate" or simply "mate." When a checking or checkmating move is made, it is customary for the player making such a move to declare "check" or "checkmate" as appropriate.

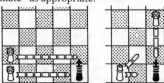

Examples of checkmate

Winning A player wins if he:
(a) checkmates his opponent's king; or
(b) forces his opponent to resign.
Checkmate may be made, or a player may resign, at
any time during the course of the game.

Drawn game Many games of chess do not end in a
victory for either player. A game is drawn in any of
the following cases.
(a) When the player whose turn it is to move can
make no legal move (a situation known as
"stalemate").
(b) When neither player has sufficient pieces to
force checkmate.
(c) When a player can check the opponent's king
indefinitely but cannot checkmate it (a situation
called "perpetual check").
(d) When no capture or pawn move has been made
by either during 50 successive moves of each player.
(e) When the same position recurs three times,
always when it is the same player's turn to move.
The right to claim a draw then belongs either to the
player who is in a position to play a move leading to
such repetition (providing that he declares his
intention of making this move), or to the player
who must reply to a move by which the repeated
position is made.
(f) When both players agree to call the game drawn.

Illegal positioning If an illegal move is made during
the course of a game, the pieces are set up as they
were just before the illegal move. If this is
impossible, the game is annulled.
If pieces are accidentally displaced and cannot be

correctly repositioned or if the initial positions of the pieces were incorrect, the game is also annulled. If the chessboard is found to have been incorrectly placed, the pieces on the board are transferred to a correctly placed board in the same position as when the error was discovered and play then continues.

Competition chess is strictly controlled. It differs from the informal game in the following ways.

(a) each player must write down every move made.

(b) Each player must make a certain number of moves in a given time (time is kept by a special control clock).

(c) If a game is adjourned, the player whose turn it is must write down his move and place it in a sealed envelope, together with his and his opponent's scoresheets. The sealed move is made on the resumption of play.

(d) It is forbidden to distract or worry an opponent; ask or receive advice from a third party; use any written or printed notes; or to analyze the game on another chessboard.

(e) A designated person must direct the competition. The competition director must ensure that the rules of play are strictly observed – he may impose penalties on any player who infringes these rules. (These notes on competition chess are an outline only. The official international governing body – the Federation Internationale des Echecs [FIDE] – lays down the full rules and interprets any problems arising in the game. Its decision is binding on all affiliated federations.)

Descriptive system: black

QR1	QKt1	QB1	Q1	K1	KB1	KKt1	KR1
QR2	QKt2	QB2	Q2	K2	KB2	KKt2	KR2
QR3	QKt3	QB3	Q3	K3	KB3	KKt3	KR3
QR4	QKt4	QB4	Q4	K4	KB4	KKt4	KR4
QR5	QKt5	QB5	Q5	K5	KB5	KKt5	KR5
QR6	QKt6	QB6	Q6	K6	KB6	KKt6	KR6
QR7	QKt7	QB7	Q7	K7	KB7	KKt7	KR7
QR8	QKt8	QB8	Q8	K8	KB8	KKt8	KR8

Chess notation is the method by which moves in a game are recorded. Two of the systems officially recognised are: the descriptive system and the algebraic system.

Descriptive system

Each piece is represented by its initial letter, but the knight may be represented by either Kt or N.

With the exceptions of the pawns and the king and queen, pieces are further distinguished by the side of the board on which they stand:

pieces to the right of the king take the prefix K;
pieces to the left of the queen take the prefix Q.

Descriptive system: white

QR8	QKt8	QB8	Q8	K8	KB8	KKt8	KR8
QR7	QKt7	QB7	Q7	K7	KB7	KKt7	KR7
QR6	QKt6	QB6	Q6	K6	KB6	KKt6	KR6
QR5	QKt5	QB5	Q5	K5	KB5	KKt5	KR5
QR4	QKt4	QB4	Q4	K4	KB4	KKt4	KR4
QR3	QKt3	QB3	Q3	K3	KB3	KKt3	KR3
QR2	QKt2	QB2	Q2	K2	KB2	KKt2	KR2
QR1	QKt1	QB1	Q1	K1	KB1	KKt1	KR1

Thus the rook to the left of the queen is a queen's rook and is represented as QR

Each file is represented by the initials of the pieces that occupy the squares at either end. The eight files (from left to right for whites, and inversely for black) are represented as follows: QR, QKt, QB, Q, K, KB, KKt, KR.

Each rank is numbered from 1 to 8; both players count from their own ends of the board. Consequently, each square has two names; one name as seen from white's side, and one from black's. For example, QKt3 (white) equals QKt6 (black).

A move is described by the initial letter of the piece
moved and the square to which it moved. For
example, the king's knight move to the third square
of the king's rook file is represented by KKt – KR3.
If two pieces of the same kind can move to the
same square, both the square from which the piece
moved and the square it arrived at are given. For
example, KKt (KB4)–KR3 means that the knight
of the fourth square of the king's bishop file made
the move, although another knight on the board
could have reached the same square in the same
move.

Other explanatory abbreviations are:

O–O or rook K denotes a castling move involving
KR;

O–O–O or rook Q denotes a castling move involving
QR;

x denotes captures;   ch or + denotes check;

1 denotes well played;   ? denotes a bad move.

Algebraic system

Each piece, with the exception of the pawns, is
represented by its initial letter (and the knights by
Kt or N). The pawns are not specially indicated.

The eight files (reading from left to right for white)
are represented by the letters from a to h.

The eight ranks (counting from white's first rank)
are numbered from 1 to 8. Initially, the white pieces
stand on ranks 1 and 2, and the black pieces on
ranks 7 and 8.

Thus each square is represented by the
combination of a letter and a number.

A move is described by the initial letter of the piece

a8	b8	c8	d8	e8	f8	g8	h8
a7	b7	c7	d7	e7	f7	g7	h7
a6	b6	c6	d6	e6	f6	g6	h6
a5	b5	c5	d5	e5	f5	g5	h5
a4	b4	c4	d4	e4	f4	g4	h4
a3	b3	c3	d3	e3	f3	g3	h3
a2	b2	c2	d2	e2	f2	g2	h2
a1	b1	c1	d1	e1	f1	g1	h1

Black (right of rows a7–h7)

White (right of rows a2–h2)

moved and the square from which it moved, plus the
square at which it arrived. For example, a bishop
moving from square f1 to square d3 is represented
by Bf1 – d3 or in a shortened from Bd3. If two
pieces of the same kind can move to the same
square, both the square from which the piece moved
and the square it arrived at are given. For example,
two knights stand on the squares f3 and g4; if the
knight on f3 makes the move to h2, the move is
written Ktf3–h2 or in the shortened form by Ktf–h2.
The other abbreviations used in the algebraic system
are the same as those for the descriptive system,
with the following additions:
: or x denotes captures;   ‡ denotes checkmate

Backgammon

Backgammon is an ancient board game developed in the Orient and now played all over the world. It is an excellent game in which the opportunities for strategic play add to the excitement of a race around the board. The fine calculation of odds involved in the skilled play has a strong attraction for the player who is prepared to gamble.

Players Only two players compete, but others may participate in the betting when games are played for money.

Pieces Each player has 15 pieces, similar to those used in Checkers. One player has dark pieces (Black) and the other light pieces (White). The pieces are variously known as "counters," "stones," or "men." In the modern game, "men" is the commonly accepted term.

Dice Each player has two dice and a cup in which to shake them.

Doubling cube In a game where players agree to bet on the outcome (there is no need to play for anything but fun), a doubling cube is used. This is a large die with faces numbered 2, 4, 8, 16, 32, 64.

Board Backgammon is played on a rectangular board divided into two halves by a "bar." One half of the board is called the "inner table" or "home table," and the other the "outer table."

Along each side of the board are marked 12 triangles, alternatively light and dark colored (this coloring has no special significance). Each triangle

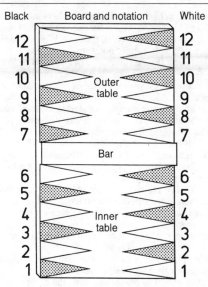

Black   Board and notation   White

Outer table

Bar

Inner table

is called a "point." For the purpose of notation, points are numbered 1 – 12 as shown in the diagram on this page. (No numbers actually appear on the board.) Points 1 (the first points in the inner table) are called "ace points;" points 7 (the first points on the outer table) are called "bar points." No other points are specially designated.

The board is place between the two players (called

Black and White) so that Black has his inner table to his right. The points on Black's side of the table are known as Black points; those on White's side as White points. In simple notation, points are indicated by their number and the initial B or W.

Objective According to the numbers thrown on the dice, each player moves his men towards his own inner table.

Once all a players men are located in his own inner table he attempts to remove them – by a process called "bearing off." The first player to bear off all 15 of his pieces wins the game.

Although the basic objective of the game is simple, the rules and strategies governing a player's moves are much more complex.

Start of play Players draw for color and then place their men in their prescribed starting positions. White places two men on B1; five men on W6; three men on W8; and five men on B12. Black places two men on W1; five men on B6; three men on B8; and five men on W12.

Having placed their men on their starting positions, each player throws a single die to determine the order of play. The player throwing the higher number has first move. If both players throw the same number they must throw again.

For his first move, the opening player moves according to the numbers on both his own and his opponent's dice. Thereafter, play alternates and each player moves according to the numbers on both his own dice.

Play A player throws both his dice to determine

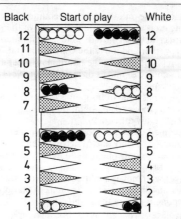

Black	Start of play	White

how many points he can move. For a valid throw
the dice must be:

thrown from the cup;

thrown in the player's own half of the board;

thrown so that one face of each die rests wholly on
the board;

thrown only when an opponent has completed his
turn.

The player then moves according to the numbers
thrown on the dice.

The direction of play for each player is always from
his opponent's inner table, through the opponent's
outer table, through his own outer table, and into
his own inner table. Thus White always moves his

men clockwise and Black moves counterclockwise.

Moving men A player attempts to move the number of points shown on each die. He may not merely add them together and move the combined total. The position of the men on the board may affect a player's choice of moves or may even prevent him from moving at all.

Provided that none of his men is off the board, a player may move to any point that is:

(a) clear of any other men;

(b) occupied by one or more of his own men; or

(c) occupied by only one of his opponent's men.

When there is only one man on a point, this man is called a "blot."

A player who moves a man to a point on which he already has one man is said to "make" that point, as his opponent cannot then land on it.

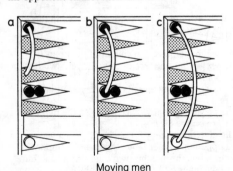

Moving men

(Also see sections on play after a mixed throw and play after a double, below and next page.)

Play after a mixed throw If the numbers on the two dice are different, the player may make one of four possible moves. For example, a player throwing a 2 and a 6 may move:

(a) one man two points, then the same man six points further;

(b) one man six points, then the same man two points further;

(c) one man two points, and another man six points;

(d) one man six points, and another man two points.

At first glance alternatives (a) and (b) appear to be the same.

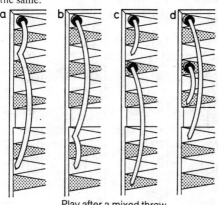

Play after a mixed throw

This is not in fact the case, since the order in which the numbers are taken can affect whether or not a man may be moved (see the section on moving men, p.228).

If he can use only the number shown on one of his dice, the other number is disregarded. If he has a choice of two numbers, he must use the higher one.

Play after a double If a player throws a double, then the number shown on both dice is played four times (or as many times as possible up to four.) Thus, if a player throws two 2s he may move:

(a) one man four times two points;

(b) one man twice two points and another man twice two points;

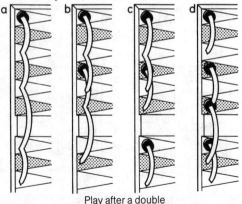

Play after a double

(c) one man twice two points and another two men two points each;

(d) four men two points each.

As before, the number shown on the dice is the limit of a move. A player moving one man four times two points must land on open points at the end of each two point move.

Hitting a man If a player moves a man onto a point on which his opponent has only one man (a) he is said to "hit" that man. The hit man is removed from play and placed on the bar (b). A player who has any hit men on the bar must re-enter them before he can move any of his men on the board.

Re-entering men To re-enter a hit man, a player must throw the number of an open point on his opponent's home table. He may then use the number on his second die to re-enter another man or, if all his men are on the board, to move any of his men the number of points shown on that die.

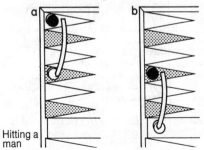

Hitting a man

Bearing off men Once a player has succeeded in moving all his men into his own inner table, he bears them off by removing them from those points corresponding to the number thrown. For example, if White throws a 4 and a 2 when he has men on both W4 and W2 he may bear off a man from each of these points.

If he throws a 4 and a 2 when he has a man on W4 but not on W2, he may bear off a man from W4 and must then move another man two points down from his highest occupied point. If he wishes, a player may always move men down the board from his highest point rather than bearing off from the points corresponding to the number on the dice.

If both numbers thrown are higher than the player's highest point, the player bears off from the highest point.

If a player's man is hit after he has started bearing off, that man must re-enter and be moved around again to the inner table before bearing off is resumed.

Bearing off continues until the player succeeds in bearing off all his men.

Fouls and penalties In addition to the rules on throwing the dice, players must observe the following:

(a) a player may not change his move after taking his hand from a moved piece;

(b) if a player makes an incorrect move, his opponent may insist that the error be corrected provided that he has not made his own following move;

(c) a game must be restarted if the board or pieces are found to be incorrectly set up during play.

Scoring The game is won by the player who first bears off all his men. The number of units scored depends on the progress of the loser:

(a) if the loser has borne off at least one man and has no men left in the winner's inner table, the winner scores one unit;

(b) if the loser has not borne off any men, the winner has made a "gammon" and scores two units;

(c) if the loser has not borne off any men and also has a man on the bar or in the winner's inner table, the winner has made a "backgammon" and scores three units.

Gambling Backgammon is often played for an agreed base stake for each game. This stake may be doubled and redoubled during play (in addition to the double payment for a gammon and treble for a backgammon). A doubling cube is often used to show the number of times that the stake has been doubled. (At the start of play it should be placed with the number 64 face uppermost.)

Unless players previously agree otherwise, stakes are automatically doubled if the dice match at the first throw of a game. In this case, both players then throw again. The number of automatic doubles is usually limited by agreement to one or two per game. There is no limit to the number of voluntary doubles.

Either player has the right to offer the first voluntary double – after which the right alternates between players. A player who wishes to double

the stake must offer to do so before throwing the
dice when it is his turn to play. His opponent then
has the choice of accepting the doubled stake or of
forfeiting the game and the stake.

Dutch
backgammon:
start

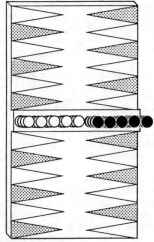

Dutch Backgammon
This is the same as the basic game except that:
(a) all the men are placed on the bar for the start of
play and players must enter all 15 before moving
any man around the board;
(b) a player may not hit a blot until he has advanced
at least one of his own men to his own inner table.

Acey Deucy

This is an elaboration of Dutch backgammon and is popular in the US Navy. It differs from the basic game in the following ways:

(a) men are entered from the bar as in Dutch backgammon;

(b) if a player throws a 1 and a 2 (ace-deuce), he moves his men for this throw and then moves his men as if he had thrown any double that he chooses;

(c) the stake is usually automatically doubled when and ace-deuce is thrown;

(d) some players give each man an agreed unit value and the winner collects as many units as the opponent has left on the board.

Gioul

This popular Middle Eastern form of Backgammon is played in the same way as the basic game except that:

(a) each player positions all his men on his opponent's number 1 point for the start;

(b) a blot is not hit but is blocked and cannot be moved while an opposing man is on the same point;

(c) when a player throws a double, he attempts to move for the double thrown and then for each subsequent double in turn up to double 6 (for example, if he throws double 4 he goes on to move for double 5 and double 6);

(d) if a player is unable to use any of his moves from a double, all these moves may be taken by his opponent.

Plakato: start

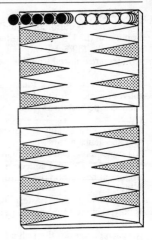

Plakato
This form of Backgammon is widely played in Greek
cafes. It is the same as the basic game described here
except that:
(**a**) each player positions all his men on his
opponent's number 1 point for the start of play;
(**b**) a blot is not hit but is blocked and cannot be
moved as long as an opposing man is on the same
point;
(**c**) a player must move all his men all 24-points
instead of bearing them off when they reach his
inner table.

Ludo

Ludo is a popular Western version of the ancient game of Parcheesi. It is a game for two, three, or four players.

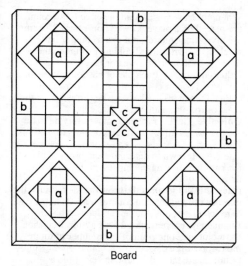

Board

(a) Home bases
(b) Starting square
(c) Finish

The board is a square-shaped piece of cardboard, marked out as shown overleaf.

The player's "home bases" and starting square, the central columns of the cross leading to the finish are the sections of the finish itself are all colored for easy identification – usually red, green, yellow and blue.

When not traveling around the circuit, the counters are placed on a player's own "home base." There are no resting squares, but one a counter has reached its own colored column leading to the finish, it cannot be followed or taken.

Other equipment Each player has four plastic or cardboard counters – of one of the board's four colors. One die is used; it may be thrown from the hand or from a small plastic dice cup.

Objective Players race each other in trying to be the first to get all four of their counters to the finish.

Play Each player chooses a set of counters.

The die is thrown to determine the order of play, the person throwing the highest number starting first.

Players take it in turns to throw the die for a 6 – the number needed to get a counter from its home base onto its starting square.

Whenever a player gets a 6 he is allowed another throw, moving one counter the number of squares indicated by the die.

Counters are moved around the circuit in a clockwise direction.

If a player has more than one counter on the circuit and he has a double throw (a 6 followed by another

throw), he may move a different counter for each
part of the throw.

Should a player throw two 6s in succession, he is
allowed a third throw.

Taking If a counter lands on a square already
occupied by an opponent's counter, the opponent's
counter must be returned to its home base and can
only re-enter the circuit on a throw of 6.

End of play The finish can only be reached by a
direct throw.

For example, if a counter is four squares away from
the finish and the player throws more than a 4, he
must either await his next throw or move one of his
other pieces.

The winner is the first player to get all four of his
counters to the finish.

Snakes and Ladders

Snakes and ladders is a development of earlier games such as the Game of goose, and has become a top favourite family game. Like many other race board games its outcome is entirely dependent on chance.

The board is divided into 100 squares. Snakes and ladders – usually about ten of each – are arranged around the board. Although the positioning of the snakes and ladders may vary from board to board, the snakes' heads are always on a higher number than their tails.

The board is often decorated with scenes of children encountering hazards or having fun.

Other equipment comprises one die and one differently colored counter for each player.

Objective Players move their counters around the board – hoping not to be "swallowed" down to a lower number by a snake and instead to be given a helping hand up a ladder to a higher number. The first player to land on the hundredth square wins the game.

Play Each player in turn moves his counter along the squares in numerical order, in accordance with the number obtained by the throw of the die.

If a player's counter lands on a square bearing the foot of a ladder, the player may move his counter up the ladder to the square at its top – thus "jumping" the intermediate squares.

If a counter lands on the head of a snake, the counter must go down the snake to the square at its tail.

End of play The game continues with players throwing the die in turn until one of them reaches the hundredth square with an exact throw.

If a player's throw is higher than the number needed for his counter to land on the last square, he has to count the difference in descending order. For example, if the counter is on square 97 and the player throws a 5, he must move forward three squares to 100 and back two squares to square 98.

Chinese checkers

Chinese checkers is a modern game derived from
Halma. It can be played by two to six persons,
playing individually or with partners.

Start of play

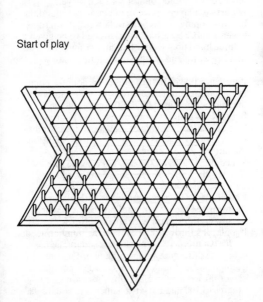

The board is made of metal, plastic, wood or cardboard. The playing areas is a six-pointed star, with holes or indentations to hold the pieces. Each of the star's points is a different color.

The pieces There are six sets of 15 pieces. Each set of the same color as one of the star's points. The most common types of pieces are plastic pegs or marbles.

Objective Players attempt to move their pieces into the opposite point. The game is won by the first player or pair to do so.

Start of play For a game between two players, each

Start: two players

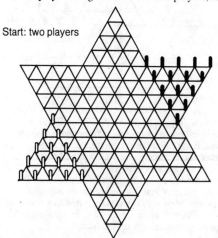

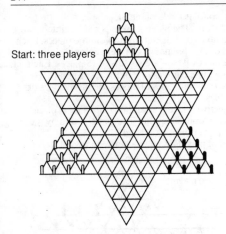

Start: three players

positions 15 pieces of appropriate colors in
opposite points of the star. When there are more
than two players, each one positions 10 pieces in
any point; partners usually take opposite points.

Turns Each player moves one piece in turn.

Moves may be made along any of the lines, i.e. in
six directions. Moves may be "steps" or "hops." A
player may hop over his own or another player's
pieces and may make several hops in one move.
Steps and hops may not be combined in a single
move. There is no compulsion to make a hop. All
hopped pieces are left on the board.

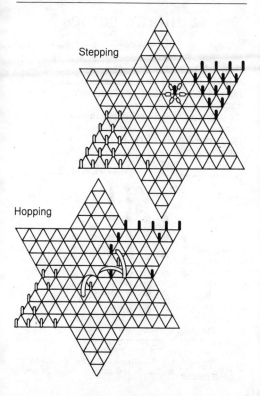

Stepping

Hopping

Solitaire games

Solitaire board games are an excellent diversion for one person. Board solitaire originated in France, where it is said to have been invented by an imprisoned nobleman. It was introduced into England in the late 1700s and has since spread to other parts of the world.

The objective of some solitaire games is to clear the board of all the pieces; in other games the player tries to position the pieces in a specific pattern.

Equipment Solitaire is played with a special board and a set of pegs or marbles made of ivory, bone, wood or plastic.

French board

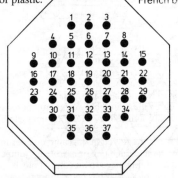

The traditional French board is octagonal and has 37 holes to accommodate the same number of pegs.

English board

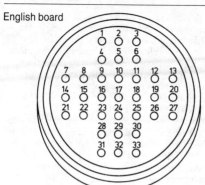

Traditional English boards are circular and have 33 hollows to hold 33 marbles. A channel running around the edge of the board holds pieces eliminated from the game.

Some solitaire games require all the pieces – others only a certain number of them. The pieces are positioned before the start of play.

(The boards illustrated have been numbered, so that the solutions to the different games can be given.)

Play Pieces are moved in the same manner in all solitaire games. Each peg or marble is "jumped" over an adjoining piece to an empty hole beyond–the piece that has been jumped over is then removed from the board. Pieces may only be moved horizontally or vertically.

Result A game is considered won only if its objective has been exactly met. For example, the standard game is a success only if the board has been completely cleared of all but one of the pieces. Although some games can be won by more than one method, a player will usually have to make numerous attempts until he has worked out a winning solution.

STANDARD SOLITAIRE

The objective of the basic solitaire game is the same whichever type of board is used. The player tries to clear the board so that at the end of the game only one piece is left – either in the central hole or in some other hole predetermined by the player.

Play start from the center of the board, after the middle piece has been removed. It is vital that no pieces are left isolated from the others during play, as they cannot then be cleared.

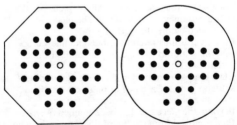

Standard solitaire: start

If the player wishes, the board can be cleared from some other chosen starting point – leaving the center hole filled and removing a piece from elsewhere on the board in order to make a starting space.

SOLITAIRE VARIANTS

There are numerous variations of the standard solitaire game, particularly for play on a French board. A player may wish to devise a variant of his own – which will require patience, persistence and plenty of time. Every move of every attempt to make a certain pattern must be noted until an exact solution has been found. The following are a selection of existing solitaire games.

THE CROSS

The cross is played using only nine pieces, positioned as shown. The object is to remove eight of the nine pieces from the board, leaving only one at the center. (The cross can be played on either the French or English board.)

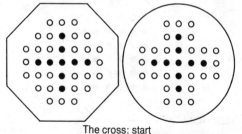

The cross: start

The corsair: start

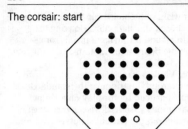

THE CORSAIR

At the start of the game all the 37 holes of a French board are filled. Any one peg at an angle of the board is then removed (i.e. 1, 3, 15, 29, 37, 35, 23, or 9).

The objective is to remove all the pieces except one – which should end up in the hole diametrically opposite the starting hole. For example, if the game was begun at hole 37 the last peg should be in hole 1.

The octagon: start

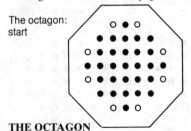

THE OCTAGON

This is another game using a French board. All the

holes except those at the angles of the board are
filled (i.e. not 1, 3, 15, 29, 37, 35, 23, and 9). The
player tries to end the game so that only one piece
– at the center of the board – remains.

PATTERN FORMING GAMES

Many pattern forming games are designed for play
on a French board. All the examples included here
begin with all 37 pieces in position. The central
piece is then removed, and the player tries to end
the game by forming the patterns shown.

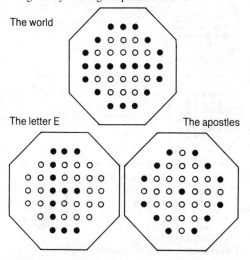

The world

The letter E

The apostles

Solutions

Standard solitaire (English)

5–17	22–24	10–8
12–10	31–23	8–2
3–11	16–28	22–24
18–6	33–31	24–26
1–3	31–23	19–17
3–11	4–16	16–18
30–18	7–9	11–25
27–25	10–8	26–24
24–26	21–7	29–17
13–27	7–9	
27–25	24–10	

Standard solitaire (French)

No known solution

The cross (English)

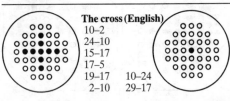

10–2	
24–10	
15–17	
17–5	
19–17	10–24
2–10	29–17

The cross (French)

12–2	21–19
26–12	2–12
17–19	12–26
19–6	32–19

The corsair

35–37	18–31	20–18
26–36	29–27	18–5
25–35	22–20	5–7
23–25	15–13	36–26
34–32	16–18	30–32
20–33	9–11	32–19
37–27	20–7	19–6
7–20	7–5	2–12
20–33	4–6	8–6
18–31	18–5	12–2
35–25	1–11	3–1
5–18	33–20	

The world

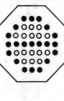

32–19	4–17
30–32	6–4
17–30	18–5
28–26	13–11
25–27	5–18
14–28	27–13
34–21	7–20
32–34	

The octagon

27–37	26–24	20–18
31–33	30–17	25–11
37–27	34–21	11–13
20–33	21–19	2–12
22–20	18–20	13–11
19–32	16–18	10–12
33–31	8–21	4–6
30–32	21–19	6–19
36–26	7–20	
17–30	11–25	

The apostles

32–19	25–27	2–7
28–26	16–18	6–8
37–27	19–17	22–20
35–37	6–19	15–13
25–35	4–6	12–14
27–25	17–4	27–13
24–26	2–12	13–15
11–25	8–6	

The letter E

32–19	7–20	
34–32	15–13	
20–33	20–7	
29–27	22–20	
33–20	6–19	
36–26	4–6	
30–32	18–5	2–12
26–36	23–25	8–6
18–31	16–17	12–2
20–18	9–11	

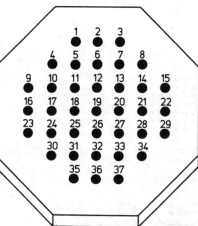